MORE
LOW-CARB
MEALS IN MINUTES

linda gassenheimer

BAY
BOOKS
SAN FRANCISCO

MORE LOW-CARB MEALS IN MINUTES

A THREE-STAGE PLAN FOR KEEPING IT OFF

linda gassenheimer

BAY BOOKS
SAN FRANCISCO

This book is dedicated to Harold for his love of good
food and his enthusiastic support for this project.

Other books by Linda Gassenheimer
French Cuisine
Simply Sauces
Keys Cuisine: Flavors of the Florida Keys
Dinner in Minutes: Memorable Meals for Busy Cooks
Vegetarian Dinner in Minutes
Low-Carb Meals in Minutes

Bay Books is an imprint of Bay/SOMA Publishing, Inc.
444 De Haro Street, No. 130, San Francisco, CA 94107.

Publisher: James Connolly
Editorial Director: Floyd Yearout
Copy-editing: Barbara King
Proofreading/Indexing: Ro Sila
Production: Jeff Brandenburg , ImageComp
Cover design: Randall Lockridge, Terrace Publishing
Book design: Mark Buckingham

Photography: Frank Wing
Food Stylist: Dina Angel-Wing

Library of Congress Cataloging-in-Publication data is on file with the Publisher.

ISBN 1-57959-523-5

Printed in Canada

10 9 8 7 6 5 4 3 2 1

Distributed by Publishers Group West

contents

foreword

Over the past decade there have been more questions than answers about whether carbohydrates are good or evil. Some diets push carbohydrates while others totally eliminate them. Finally, results of recent nutrition research on a common hormone condition, insulin resistance, offers the right answer for many. This condition affects almost half of all Americans and an even higher percent of those who are overweight.

Inherited as a survival gene, insulin resistance provided a way for our hunter/gatherer ancestors to efficiently store fat and survive a famine. People with insulin resistance produce higher-than-normal amounts of insulin after eating carbohydrates. This promotes an increase in fat storing. Modern-day food manufacturing technology and the rarity of famines in Western culture have resulted in an overabundance of low-cost, good-tasting, super-refined starchy and sugary foods. Our ancient genetic hardwiring has not been able to keep up with cultural modernization. As a result, insulin resistance is now the root cause of our "lifestyle diseases," replacing its previous role in promoting survival.

Eating carbohydrates in excess causes repeated demands for more and more insulin. High insulin levels accelerate obesity. This phenomenon explains the obesity pandemic threatening both adults and children in this country. Abnormally high insulin levels also cause serious detriments to every organ of the body. Insulin resistance promotes heart attacks and strokes because it causes high blood pressure, abnormal cholesterol levels, atherosclerosis, and blood clotting disorders. Insulin resistance precedes every case of adult-onset diabetes. Polycystic ovarian syndrome (PCOS), the most common cause of female infertility and hormone dysfunction, is now recognized as originating from insulin resistance.

The National Institutes of Health (NIH) have cited insulin resistance as the "epidemic of the modern era." Unfortunately, most people don't know they have insulin resistance. The NIH has issued a plea to health professionals to aggressively screen for it. The condition is very easy to treat and all the associated disease processes can be eliminated. The treatment starts with modifying our American diet.

If carbohydrates aggravate insulin resistance, then wouldn't the solution be to eliminate all carbohydrates? Indeed, severe carbohydrate restriction has been the dieting hype this past decade. Besides being totally unrealistic, impractical, and a proven disaster for long-term weight loss, carbohydrate deprivation is also not without its cost to health. Inadequate carbohydrate intake leads to depression, fatigue, mood instability, and sleep disturbances.

My medical experience in treating 5,000 weight-loss patients over the past seven years (almost all of whom had insulin resistance) has proven that eating carbohydrates is not only possible but is recommended to maintain proper physical and mental health. The key to properly eating carbohydrates is in knowing which kinds and amounts can be comfortably tolerated without causing an abnormal insulin response.

Linda's *Low-Carb Meal's in Minutes* books have been a valuable resource for my patients. Her nutritional information aligns with our medical philosophy about insulin resistance. I commend her efforts to include all the food groups — protein, carbohydrates, and fats — in all her menu formats. Her consist simplicity in food preparation is especially appreciated. No treatment is more doomed than expecting someone to follow a complicated, restrictive, elaborate, time-consuming dietary regimen.

Her shopping lists provide the detail necessary to improve efficiency and her menu plans help eliminate unnecessary guesswork. I find her recipe format with nutritional value listings extremely helpful, especially the unusual but important information on saturated fat and fiber content.

An especially wonderful feature of Linda's books is her gourmet recipes for entertaining. The freedom of creating and serving one of Linda's culinary feasts completely eliminates the social isolation often felt during dieting It's hard to believe the recipes are so healthy. I actually write prescriptions for my patients to get these books. Linda's *Low-Carb Meals in Minutes* and *More Low-Carb Meals in Minutes* are consistent with my medical philosophy about what food should be: simple, snappy, scientifically sound, and scrumptious.

More Low-Carb Meals in Minutes is a successful blend of healthful dining and gastronomic gusto— simply, one of life's great pleasures. Enjoy.

A Salute To Your Health,
Cheryle R. Hart, M.D.
Author of *The Insulin Resistance Diet*

introduction

Seven years ago my husband came home from a visit to the cardiologist and said, "My doctor wants me to go on a low-carbohydrate diet." His triglycerides were high and climbing and he was having trouble losing the few pounds he had gained on vacation. This was a new challenge for me. I didn't want to go the route of gimmick eating: no eating all the eggs and bacon you want or eating at certain times of the day or with certain food combinations. On the other hand, as I watched him struggle to put together low-carb meals, I realized that this was going to be a challenge for both of us. Bagels for breakfast and cans of sugary sodas after tennis were out. No more baked potato with his steak. And what could he substitute for crackers and chips with drinks? I wanted a real eating lifestyle that fit our busy lives, our eating out, and entertaining. Most of all I wanted good food that was good for us, too.

I worked with two cardiologists, an endocrinologist, and nutritionists to create an eating lifestyle that was healthy and balanced. What I found was that the doctors and nutritionists could readily explain why this approach worked but could not tell me how to adapt it to my busy life. In fact, when I attended medical lectures with these doctors, the reception for the diet was highly enthusiastic, but the questions at the end — even from the doctors in the audience — were "How do I do it? What do I eat?" The recipes I created had to be low in carbohydrates, use lean proteins and monounsaturated fats (olive and canola oil), and most of all, be delicious. The result was my book, *Low-Carb Meals in Minutes,* which was so well received it reached number one on Amazon.com's bestseller list.

What prompted me to write this sequel was the incredible response from readers:

"Your cookbook *Low-Carb Meals in Minutes* was truly an inspiration to me, and I attribute most of my weight loss of 30 pounds to using your healthful and delicious recipes (husband pleasers as well). Thank you for your wonderful contributions to keeping us well fed in such a healthful manner."

"Although you have likely heard this a million times, your book is outstanding. I must own close to 50–75 cookbooks I've collected over the years. The way you organized your book with shopping lists and cooking tips, yours is among my favorites."

"I decided to buy your *Low-Carb Meals in Minutes* cookbook after seeing you on *Cooking Live*. I was a little concerned about the number of carbohydrates I was eating, plus I was borderline for gestational diabetes while I was pregnant. I really want to avoid getting adult-onset diabetes, so I thought a low-carb diet would be my best bet."

"I just want to let you know how well-organized the cookbook is, and how tasty all of the recipes are. I am always very satisfied by the meals. I am still in the Quick Starts phase of the book, but have found that the recipes are so varied. I'm surprised that my husband also enjoys them! I see it more as a change in my diet, rather than being 'on' a diet. The way your meals are set up forces me to plan things out, and not resort to 'quick' fixes. Thanks again for putting together a great cookbook!"

"So many of your menus are part of my daily repertoire now. Tonight we enjoyed 'grilled scallops parmigiana'—wonderful! I have tried to plan low-carb meals for three years but with a full-time job as a high school foods teacher (which diminishes my desire to cook!) and other obligations, I found that what my husband and I were eating was boring: grilled chicken or fish, vegetables and salad, dinners out or fast food. I know what to do and how to do it but it takes time— you have done all the planning and all I have to do after a day's work is to stop by the seafood market or grocery and I can have a good-tasting meal in a half hour or less! What I have enjoyed most are the sauces that accompany the poultry or fish which deliver great flavor. I have discovered that I must prep all ingredients before starting as the cooking is so quick! My best weeks have been when I have shopped for a whole week and have no decisions about what to make for dinner. As a fan who has a folder of 'Dinner in Minutes' from the *Miami Herald*, I was so happy to find out that you wrote a low-carb cookbook and look forward to your next one."

"My husband and I took part in an office competition to lose weight. We used your book and my husband lost 30 pounds and I've lost 20. And I've talked to all of my friends about it. We love the recipes. Thanks."

"I started using your book, although I was skeptical about low carbohydrates Atkin's-type diet as many in the office thought a Slim Jim & Cheese was acceptable. I'm down 20 pounds following your guidelines. Thanks."

"Your book is exactly what I've been looking for. My husband is an endocrinologist and has advised his patients about many of the things you discussed on *Cooking Live*."

"We bought two copies of *Low-Carb Meals in Minutes* and gave one to our daughter and son-in-law. Our particular favorite is the chocolate soufflé dessert. It is hard for me to believe that something so delicious is not negative for health."

"My husband has high blood pressure and high cholesterol and we are looking for a good diet to follow. This one is the right ticket. Have tried the recipes and love them."

"So far *Low-Carb Meals in Minutes* has been great for my husband and me because we used to get tired of eating the same things over and over and we never ate healthy foods. Now we are eating much healthier."

Low-Carb Meals in Minutes is a three-step program to losing weight and keeping it off. The first, Quick Start, is a two-week menu that jump-starts quick weight loss. Which Carbs is the next two-week step that gradually reintroduces carbohydrates into the menu while you are still losing weight. The final phase, Right Carbs, is a balanced menu that shows how to eat the right carbohydrates and keep the weight off. *More Low-Carb Meals* in Minutes gives an entirely new two weeks of meals for each of these phases.

A new feature in this book is a Super Speed Supper section containing even quicker dinners for busy weeknights based on buying partially prepared ingredients from the supermarket. The supermarkets have come a long way in helping us get our meals on the table in minutes. For those nights when you want to get dinner ready in 15 minutes, this section has meals based on ingredients bought in the supermarket that can be quickly assembled at home into a meal that fits our guidelines.

Another feature is a Weekends section containing meals that are a little special when you have some additional time. You can enjoy weekend meals and not feel that dreaded Monday morning I-have-to-be-good syndrome.

I have also answered the question of how to entertain within the eating lifestyle with five different parties in the Entertaining section. I have created meals that won't break the carb or calorie scale. I had some friends over for dinner and they called the next day to say how much they loved the food but were afraid to get on the scale after having seconds. I told them to forget the scale. All of the foods fit the low-carb guidelines, and they didn't have to worry. They couldn't believe it. The Entertaining section here is filled with this style of food. From football parties to a casual dinner with friends to an elegant dinner for eight, you can choose whichever menu suits your needs. And don't tell your guests the food is low-carb or healthy and they'll just enjoy the fun. Finding the time to shop and cook for friends can be difficult these days. The parties in this section use ingredients that can be bought in one-stop shopping at the local supermarket. The recipes take minutes to make and many can be made ahead. I give you a shopping list and countdown explaining how far in advance the recipe can be made, how to store it, and how to rewarm and serve it.

While producing my National Public Radio program at WLRN in Miami, I was surprised that several of the men there were trying to cut back on their carbohydrates. Their first questions were, "What's on the list?" and "What's off the list?"

I myself was lost when I first tried to make low-carbohydrate meals. I had to fundamentally rethink my approach to shopping and cooking. I started by restocking the pantry and refrigerator. The changes were dramatic.

Off the list were

- Low-fat processed foods such as fat-free cookies and cakes and other sugary desserts
- Fat-free mayonnaise, salad dressings, cream cheese, and sour cream
- Condiments, sauces, and salsas where sugar is one of the first five ingredients
- Pancakes, bagels, and waffles
- Jams and jellies
- Pizza and platefuls of pasta as a main course
- Garnished baked potato as a meal
- Sugary sodas and fruit juices
- Chips, pretzels, and popcorn

On the list were

- Eggs, as many as four a week (We hadn't eaten them for breakfast for 10 years.)
- Egg substitute (which is basically egg whites), as a good source of protein
- A well-stocked vegetable drawer, including cucumbers, lettuce, celery, bell peppers, mushrooms, and tomatoes
- Lean deli meats such as turkey breast, chicken, ham, and roast beef

- Brown rice and whole wheat pasta, in place of the lower fiber, less nutritious white varieties
- High-fiber, whole-grain breads that are relatively low in carbs
- No-sugar-added tomato sauce and salad dressings
- Real mayonnaise made with soybean or olive oil
- High-fiber, no-sugar-added bran cereal for breakfast
- Olive and canola oil
- Walnuts, pecans, almonds, and peanuts
- Eight glasses (64 ounces) of water per day

With this list of do's and don'ts, I created recipes that are fast, fun, and delicious. My husband's response was enthusiastic: He lost weight, has kept it off for seven years, and lowered his blood cholesterol and triglyceride counts to healthy levels.

Why is this lifestyle becoming mainstream in American eating? Why are millions of people giving up their bagels, sandwiches, and pasta meals? After unsuccessful attempts at weight loss from low-fat, high-carb diets, they're finally getting the results they want from a low-carb lifestyle. What are the principles behind it and why is it working for so many people?

In a nutshell, the theory behind low-carbohydrate diets is this: Eating lots of carbohydrates over-stimulates insulin production, causing peaks and valleys in blood sugar levels that, in turn, create hunger pangs. On the other hand, protein is digested more slowly, promoting more even blood sugar levels. Eating more protein, fewer carbs, and more monounsaturated fat promotes weight loss by decreasing fat storage, increasing fat burning, and delaying the onset of hunger pangs.

The major low-carbohydrate books, such as *The Zone, Protein Power, Sugar Busters, Dr. Atkins' New Diet Revolution,* and *The Carbohydrate Addict's Diet,* differ in their approaches, but their central idea is to use diet to moderate insulin levels for the reasons explained above. All of the recipes in this book fit into the low-carbohydrate guidelines outlined in these books (and others on the subject).

Several cardiologists steered me away from diets that call for high levels of saturated fat. The menus in this book are similar to a Mediterranean-style diet using fresh vegetables, monounsaturated olive and canola oils, and lean meats and fish.

These meals follow the same guidelines as my syndicated *Dinner in Minutes* columns: attractive, delicious, fun, healthful, "no brainer" meals that are quick and easy to make. All the breakfast, lunch, and dinner menus are presented as entire meals, so you don't have to think about how to cook a dish or what goes with what.

I developed these techniques after many years of juggling my family, career (founding and running a cooking school, guiding a gourmet supermarket as its executive director, writing a food column for newspapers and magazines, and hosting a radio talk show), and a desire for good food.

It's a method that covers all aspects from purchasing and preparing ingredients to presenting complete meals.

My *Dinner in Minutes* columns have simple, easy-to-follow recipes. From years of training, I've learned to use classic techniques and familiar combinations to produce delicious results while cutting the cooking time.

It's a blueprint that can be used for everyday meals or dressed up for parties or special occasions.

Special Features

Shopping List

The *More Low-Carb Meals in Minutes* blueprint contains a shopping list based on how the food is bought in the market.

- Quick shopping is as important as quick cooking. You won't have to think about how many mushrooms to buy. I've given you the amount.

- I list the ingredients by supermarket departments to help you navigate the aisles with ease.

- I've included tips on how to get in and out of the supermarket fast and how to take advantage of today's timesaving prepared foods.

- The staples list helps you organize your cabinets so that they are not filled with extraneous items. To help you plan your pantry, I have included a separate section using the staples listed in the book. You will already have many of the ingredients for the recipes and only need to buy a few fresh items.

- My 15-year-old *Dinner in Minutes* syndicated column is known as the one with the shopping list. People have told me that the list saves them both time and money because they buy only what they need.

Shopping Guidelines

Many of the recipes call for prepared condiments such as salad dressings, pasta sauce, Chinese sauces, and others.

- There are many brands to choose from. To help you pick the ones that will fit the nutritional guidelines, I have added a section that tells you what to look for on the nutritional labels of the products.

- Find the products that you like best and keep them on hand so you won't have to think about which one to use.

Helpful Hints and Countdown

Each meal contains helpful hints on shopping, cooking, and substitutions, as well as a countdown so you can get the whole meal on the table at the same time.

- You can hit the kitchen on the run without having to plan or think about each step.

- In my home, the dinner preparation encompasses the time I turn on the light in the kitchen until the plates are brought to the table.

- The helpful hints tell you what to buy, how to buy, and what you can substitute. They include tips on the best preparation method and quick-cooking techniques, as well as timesaving cleanup tips.

- *More Low-Carb Meals in Minutes* doesn't mean broiled chicken every night. You will find a wide variety of delicious meals covering many ethnic flavors.

- As you eat through this book, you can enjoy a Tuscan Chicken and Tomato-Basil Relish and Toasted Almond Broccoli; Five-Spice Tuna Tataki with Japanese Brown Rice and Raspberry Banana Cooler; Whiskey-Soused Salmon with Broccoli and Potatoes and Deep Dish Blueberry Cream; Mahi Mahi Satay with Thai Peanut Sauce, Snow Peas, Rice, and Lychee Cup; and Mexican Sopes (Layered Open Tortilla Sandwich) and Oranges in Cherry Coulis. Wherever I travel throughout the world, I go to street markets with chefs, taste their foods, and bring back their flavors to add to the repertoire of simple, low-carb recipes.

Flexibility

A blueprint means that preparation is totally flexible.

- When you choose a fish recipe, you can buy the freshest-looking fish in the market rather than the fish called for in the recipe.

- You can use the best sirloin, filet, strip steak, or more economical cuts like flank and skirt steaks.

- All of the recipes were tested to produce delicious results with products found in one-stop shopping at your local supermarket.

- Branching out to use the freshest and best ingredients—like a favorite gourmet infused olive oil or aged balsamic vinegar—will add even more flavor and zip to these recipes.

- You can use the ingredients called for or change them within the blueprint guidelines to suit your taste. My recipes call for lean ham, turkey, and roast beef. You can create fun, tempting, endless variations by using Black Forest ham, Cajun roast beef, or mesquite-smoked turkey breast.

- This flexible approach lets you choose whatever is in season, on the shelf, or just fits your mood.

As I mentioned above, this low-carbohydrate lifestyle is divided into three phases: an initial phase of significant carbohydrate reduction, an intermediate phase for reintroduction of carbs, and a maintenance phase of balanced eating.

QUICK START — The first step to a successful eating plan calls for a reduction of carbohydrates. While differences exist, most proponents advise a level of about 30 to 40 grams of carbs a day. My Quick Start section maintains that level through healthy recipes containing vegetables and lean proteins.

WHICH CARBS — Carbohydrates are an important nutrient and the second step reintroduces high-fiber, low-simple-sugar carbohydrates at a level permitting continuing weight loss. Listening to the questions from the participants in my low-carb classes, I realized the second phase is the most difficult. They are afraid that returning to higher levels of carbohydrates will negate all of the benefits they've achieved.

RIGHT CARBS — The third stage leaves you permanently with the Right Carbs. So, what should you eat to maintain your weight loss? Right Carbs has the answers. This section achieves a well-balanced lifestyle of approximately 40 percent calories from carbohydrates, 30 percent calories from lean proteins, and 30 percent calories from fat (primarily monoun-saturated).[1]

So how does my husband handle vacations and blow-out weekends? No need to worry here. Remember, balance is the key. We have found that you can splurge on special occasions without negative effects when you come back to the Right Carbs. In fact, one cardiologist advisor said that varying from a good base once in a while still leaves you much better off than if you don't have that base at all. In other words, the low-carbohydrate approach is forgiving. Following the program even with some deviations will produce a good result. My husband found that returning to the Right Carbs is easy because it takes so little effort and the menus are so appealing. Any time you want to restart weight loss, you can go back to Quick Start for a week or two and work yourself back up to Right Carbs.

More Low-Carb Meals in Minutes is for all of you who want to eat healthfully and fit a low-carbohydrate weight-loss program into your time-starved lives. The low-carb lifestyle has certainly changed our lives. My husband and I no longer think about what is and isn't low-carb—we just consider it good food that fits into our busy schedules.

Before you start a program of this type, it is always best to check with your doctor first. This is especially true if you are taking any medication under a doctor's care. If your doctor recommends a blood test, it will provide a baseline against which to compare your results.

These meals have been made by my many students and readers from all over the United States. Wherever I travel and lecture, they tell me how well the plans work. I get hundreds of emails on how well readers are doing and how these easy meals have changed their lives. They love the variety that comes from my travels around the world. My goal in sharing these recipes with you is to help you enjoy good food for good health. My husband and I love good food. Now, with these recipes, we can live to eat and eat to live. We hope you enjoy them, too. Bon appétit.

---

[1] Why 40-30-30? All foods contain only these three components (carbohydrates, protein, and fat) and all are essential for your well-being. While there are differences of opinion, diet experts generally agree that fat levels (primarily monounsaturated) should make up 30 percent of one's diet. Carbohydrate intake should be restricted to 30 percent more than protein intake. So, if the calories from protein are 30% of diet, the correct carbohydrate level should be 40%.

Smart Shopping the Low-Carb Way

"I hate to shop. I'd cook more if I had the ingredients at home," is a comment I hear often. Here are some tips that will help get you in and out of the market quickly. It should help you beat the I-hate-to-shop syndrome.

Some Advice

The adage of "Don't go to the store hungry" is true. It can be a disaster. If I go to the market when I'm tired and hungry, I just get to a starving point and eat anything offered to me. Shop after a meal or have a snack before you go. This will help you concentrate on what you should be buying instead of what you shouldn't buy.

Try to go to the market when it isn't crowded or directly after you've put in a long day's work. Carry a cooler in your car so you can stop on the way to work, during lunch, or at other times. (The cooler will protect foods from moderate heat and cold. It won't help with extreme heat or freezing temperatures.)

Many offices have refrigerators. If one is available to you, shop before work or at lunch and store your food in the refrigerator. Here's a hint: There have been many times when I've left my packages at work or at a friend's house. The best solution to this is to put your car keys in one of the shopping bags. You won't be able to go anywhere without them.

Keep the foods from my staples list on hand. (See pages 23–25.) You will only need to pick up a few fresh items to complete your meal.

Supermarket Savvy: Let the Markets Help You

Supermarkets are constantly updating their product mix to help us get our meals on the table fast. Use the supermarket to your advantage.

Salad Bars

These are great for picking up a quick salad or lunch and for buying cut vegetables and fruits for cooking at home.

Deli

Look at the nutritional information label to choose the new, leaner cuts of cooked meats. Canadian bacon, roast beef, and ham have been made leaner and without high carbs.

Dairy

Reduced-fat cheese has come a long way. Gone is the rubbery cheese that won't melt. Many brands using new techniques have developed lower-fat cheese that melt well and are full of flavor.

Prepared Foods

Ask for roast chicken breast only. Ask for an ingredients list. Read the labels carefully for all prepared foods. Many have added salt and sugar. Many prepared sauces and condiments are now made in a low-salt, low-carbohydrate version. Look for these in the market. (See page 21 for Shopping Guidelines.)

Produce Department

Bags of washed, ready-to-eat salads have been one of the best conveniences I've seen. Read the labels. If they don't say ready-to-eat or washed, then you will need to wash the ingredients prior to using.

Shredded carrots, lettuce, and coleslaw mixtures are another big help to getting meals on the table in minutes.

Many supermarkets have cubes of melons and pineapple ready to eat.

Meat Department

Look for lower fat or lean meats. Many markets now have separate sections for lean meats or mark them with special labels. Pork and beef are now available with reduced-fat content.

There are many marinated or precooked meats available. Watch for sugar, salt, and fat content.

Roasted chicken breast, strips, and pieces are available. The ones without skin or honey sauces are perfect for salads, sandwiches, and soups.

Grocery Aisles

There are many items that make our lives easier and more are coming out each day. Low-fat, no-sugar-added tomato sauce, pasta sauces, and salad dressings are a few of the products. In fact, there are so many available, it's best to try a few and, when you find one you like, keep a few bottles on hand. Most important is to read the nutritional labels and ingredients lists. (See page 21 for the Shopping Guidelines.)

How to Read the Labels

When you're shopping, it's worth a few extra minutes to read the food labels. They can be confusing. Here are some answers to the most frequently asked questions.

What do "reduced fat," "low fat," and "light" on a label mean?

- "Low fat" means 3 grams of fat or fewer per serving.
- "Reduced fat" means at least 25 percent less fat per serving than the regular version of the same food.

- "Sugar free," according to the FDA, must contain fewer than 0.5 gram per serving.
- "Light" generally means that the food contains 50 percent fewer calories from fat than the regular version of the same food.

Check the serving size on the label. It can be misleading. If the serving size is 1 tablespoon, you need to think if that is the amount you will actually eat.

Ingredients must be listed in descending order by weight. Generally, if an ingredient is fifth or lower in the list, it has minimal amounts in each serving.

Shopping Guidelines

Throughout the book I use prepared products from the supermarket. There are many brands that will fill the bill. On the other hand, there is considerable variation in the contents of these products. The best advice is to find the product that fits the nutritional analysis and has the best flavor. Once you've found one you prefer, keep it on hand.

Here are some guidelines on what to look for on the nutritional labels:

Oil and Vinegar Dressing, Balsamic Dressing, Vinaigrettes

The nutritional analysis for meals using one of these ingredients is based on olive oil or canola oil dressings. Try to stay away from nonfat dressings. In general when they cut the fat, they add carbohydrates.

Look for:

Quantity	Calories	Carbohydrates
1 tablespoon	75	0.5–1.5 g

Mayonnaise

Look for:

Soybean oil, canola oil, or olive oil (Major brands are made with soybean oil.)

Quantity	Calories	Carbohydrates
1 tablespoon	100	0 g

Reduced-Fat Mayonnaise

Look for:

Quantity	Calories	Carbohydrates	Fat
1 tablespoon	50	1 g	5 g

Caesar Dressing

Look for:

Quantity	Calories	Carbohydrates
1 tablespoon	80	0.5–1.5 g

Tomato and Pasta Sauces

Look for no-sugar-added, no-salt-added, or low-sodium brands. There are many excellent ones to choose from.

Look for:

Qty	Calories	Carbs	Fiber	Sodium	Fat
1 cup	60–80	12–14 g	2–3 g	40 mg	0 g

Nonfat, Low-Sodium Chicken Broth

Look for:

Quantity	Calories	Sodium
1 cup	15	560 mg

Low-Sodium Soy Sauce

Look for:

Quantity	Calories	Sodium
1 tablespoon	10	574 mg

Lite Teriyaki Sauce

Look for:

Quantity	Calories	Sodium
1 tablespoon	15	320 mg

Tortilla

Look for:

Quantity	Calories	Carbohydrates
6-inch tortilla weighing 1 oz.	90	16 g

Whole Wheat Bread

Look for:

Quantity	Calories	Carbohydrates	Fiber
1 slice	50	10 g	3 g

Other Breads and Rolls

Look for:

Quantity	Calories	Carbohydrates	Fiber
1 slice/1 roll	80	15 g	0.7–2 g

Cereal: Fiber One*

Look for:

Quantity	Calories	Carbohydrates	Fiber
1/2 cup	60	24 g	13 g

Cereal: All-Bran and Bran Buds*

Look for:

Quantity	Calories	Carbohydrates	Fiber
1/3 cup	80	24 g	13 g

*For cereals: Read labels carefully; labels say they're healthy, but you need to look for the amounts of sugar, molasses, corn syrup, or honey.

Lean Ham and Canadian Bacon

Look for:

Quantity	Calories	Sodium	Fat
1 ounce	37	246 mg	1.4 g

Reduced-Fat, Part-Skim Milk Mozzarella Cheese

Look for:

Quantity	Calories	Sodium	Fat
1 ounce	72	132 mg	4.5 g

Pimientos

Look for:

Quantity	Calories	Carbohydrates	Fat	Sodium
1 cup	40	8 g	0 g	20 mg

Marinated Artichoke Hearts

Look for:

Quantity	Calories	Carbohydrates	Fat	Sodium
1 ounce	25	2 g	1.5 g	90 mg

Unsweetened Applesauce

Look for:

Quantity	Calories	Carbohydrates	Sodium
1 cup	100	30 g	30 mg

Low-Fat Frozen Yogurt

Look for:

Quantity	Calories	Fat	Carbohydrates
½ cup	120	3 g	20 g

Staples

This is a comprehensive list of the staples listed in the recipes included in this book. Keep these staples on hand and you'll only need to pick up a few fresh items to make quick meals.

Canned or Bottle Goods

No-sugar-added oil (olive or canola) and
   vinegar dressing

Canned tuna packed in water

Low-sodium tomato or V-8 juice

Low-sodium, no-sugar-added tomato sauce and
   diced tomatoes

No-sugar-added tomato salsa

Mayonnaise made with olive or soybean oil

Reduced-fat mayonnaise

Fat-free, low-salt chicken broth

Dijon mustard

Canned chickpeas, black beans, navy beans,
   cannellini (white kidney) beans, red kidney beans

Condiments

Worcestershire sauce

Hot pepper sauce

Low-sodium soy sauce

Dairy

Parmesan cheese

Light yogurt

Skim milk

Eggs

Egg substitute

Butter

Dry Goods

Quick-cooking pearl barley

Lentils

Whole wheat pasta

Whole wheat flour

High-fiber, no-sugar-added bran cereal

Oatmeal

Salt

Cornstarch

Sugar substitute

Freezer Goods

Frozen chopped onion

Frozen diced green pepper

Grains and Breads

100% whole wheat bread

Rye bread

Multigrain bread

Whole wheat pita bread

Whole wheat tortilla

Barley

Lentils

Brown rice (30-minute quick-cooking and
    10-minute quick-cooking)

Wild rice

Oils and Vinegars

Olive oil

Canola oil

Olive oil spray

Balsamic vinegar

Rice vinegar

Distilled white vinegar

Red wine vinegar

Produce Department

Carrots

Celery

Garlic

Lemon

Red onions

Yellow onions

Spices and Herbs

Black peppercorns

Cayenne pepper

Chili powder

Dried oregano

Dried rosemary

Dried thyme

Dried tarragon

Dried dill

Dried ground sage

Freeze-dried chives

Ground cumin

Ground cinnamon

Ground nutmeg

Equipment

You really don't need a lot of special equipment to make these meals. However, here's a list of some items that will speed your preparation and cooking and make your life easier.

Food Processor

A food processor or mini-chopper will help quickly slice and chop and also blend foods together.

Garlic Press

Some of the newer ones allow you to crush garlic without peeling the cloves. I also use it to crush fresh ginger.

Knives

Sharp knives are important for fast and accurate cutting. A dull knife can be dangerous. It can slip or slide when you are trying to slice. Three different types are all you really need for most cutting tasks: a 4-inch paring knife, an 8-inch chef's knife, and a small serrated knife for fruit or tomatoes.

Meat Thermometer

I love the new style that uses a probe. The cord is connected to a dial that sits on the counter. The dial is easy to read and doesn't get hot or dirty. With the cord, it works well for items on the stove, in the oven, or on the grill.

Microwave Ovens

Use this fast-cooking appliance. And remember, any dish that's microwave safe is dishwasher safe, too. Be careful; it's easy to overcook food. Food continues to cook several seconds after it has been removed from the oven.

Pots and Pans

You can make most of the meals in this book using a medium (9- to10-inch) nonstick skillet, a large (3- to 4-quart) saucepan, and a wok. Nonstick skillets are essential as these recipes use small amounts of oil. If you follow the instructions, your food will not stick.

Scale

A small kitchen scale is very handy and not expensive. Where weights are given, I've also listed measurements in cups and ounces, though it's much faster and more accurate to use a scale.

Vegetable Peeler

For easy peeling, make sure yours is sharp. These are actually little knives and should be replaced as they start to dull.

Quick Cooking Tips and Helpful Hints

Each recipe has a Helpful Hints section. Knowing what to substitute, the best way to prepare ingredients, or some other shortcut can make a big difference in the time it takes you to get your meal on the table.

Slices and Weight

To determine the weight of sliced cheese or packaged meats, look at the package weight or nutritional analysis to determine how much each slice weighs.

Parmesan Cheese

Buy good-quality Parmesan cheese and ask the market to grate it for you or chop it in the food processor. Freeze extra for quick use later. You can quickly spoon out what you need and leave the rest frozen.

Washing Mushrooms

To clean whole mushrooms, wipe them with a damp paper towel.

Washing Herbs

The quickest way to wash watercress, arugula, parsley, or basil is to place the bunch, head first, into a bowl of water. Leave it for a minute, then lift it out and shake dry. The dirt and sand will be left behind.

Chopping Fresh Herbs

To quickly chop herbs, snip the leaves right off the stem with scissors.

Fresh Ginger

To chop fresh ginger quickly, cut it into small cubes and press through a garlic press with large holes. If using a press with small holes, just capture the juice that is squeezed out; it will give enough flavor for the recipe.

Dried Spices and Herbs

If using dried spices, make sure they are less than 6 months old. To bring out the flavor of the dried herbs, chop them with fresh parsley. The juice from the parsley will help release the flavor of the herbs.

Shelling Shrimp

Buy shelled, deveined shrimp or ask for the shrimp to be shelled for you while you complete your shopping. Most stores will do this for a small fee, which is worth the time saved in shelling and deveining them yourself.

Food Processor

To use the food processor for a recipe without having to stop to wash the bowl, first chop the dry ingredients (such as nuts), and then the wet ones (such as onion). You won't have to stop in the middle of preparing the ingredients.

Crisp Stir-Fry

For crisp, not steamed, stir-fried vegetables, make sure your wok or skillet is very hot. The oil should be smoking. Let the vegetables sit a minute before tossing to allow the wok to regain its heat.

Timely Stir-Fry

To keep from looking back at a recipe as you stir-fry the ingredients, line them up on a cutting board or plate in the order of use. You will know which ingredient comes next.

Electric Cooking

To get a quick high/low response from electric burners, heat two burners, one on medium-high and the other on low. Move the pot back and forth between them.

Fluffy Rice

I like to cook my rice like pasta, using a large enough saucepan of boiling water for the rice to roll freely; strain when cooked. You also can follow the directions on the rice package.

Tips for Eating Out

One of the biggest challenges to making sure we eat healthfully is that 60 percent of our meals are prepared outside the home. We eat out, bring in, and eat on the run. Use the recipes in this book as a guide to eating out. Once you understand the types of food and proportion sizes, you will be able to order from a menu with confidence. Here are some hints and tips to eat well in spite of your schedule:

- Avoid all deep fried foods.
- Avoid sugary drinks. Opt for water, unsweetened ice tea, or diet soda.
- Plain, soft tacos or tortilla-filled wraps are fine as long as they aren't filled with rice and beans. Ask for whole wheat tortillas, if possible.
- Roasted or grilled meats are best. Make sure you include vegetables with your meal. Stay away from sugar-based sauces, especially barbecue sauce and most glazes.
- Many meals are loaded with carbs. Order two vegetables instead of a starch. Most restaurants are used to substituting this way.
- Ask for your salad dressing on the side. Most salads come swimming in dressing. You'll be surprised how far 1 tablespoon of dressing will go. Or just lightly dip your vegetables into the dressing on the side.
- If you order dessert, share it with the table or make sure you don't have a starch during dinner. Better still, order a fresh fruit salad or berries.
- Have a low-carb snack (vegetables, a few nuts, a slice of low-carbohydrate cheese) before you go out to eat. This will help you avoid the basket of bread on the table while you're waiting for your meal.

- Ask for the bread basket to be brought to the table with the main course to save munching on the bread while you are ordering.

- Don't go out for drinks or attend a cocktail party on an empty stomach. One drink on an empty stomach will make you immediately hungry and you'll eat the first thing you can find. Have a healthy snack before you go out. (See page 30 for a snack list.) If you think it will be a long cocktail hour, start with sparkling water with a piece of lemon or lime or a diet soda. Then go on to a drink or glass of wine.

- Fast food can be fine. Order grilled chicken or fish and discard the bread or roll. Or eat it as an open sandwich using just one half of the roll. Order a salad with the dressing on the side. Stay away from fries, baked potatoes, and chips.

- Chinese food can be loaded with sugar. Order stir-fried meats and vegetables or skewered meats. Avoid soups with wontons. Avoid egg rolls, ribs in thick sauce, and noodles. It is refreshing to see that some restaurants are offering brown rice as an alternative to white rice.

- Italian food doesn't have to mean a plate of pasta. Order an antipasto platter or any of the meats, salads, or vegetables.

- French food can be very healthy. Order clear soups, salads, vegetables, meats, or seafood, but avoid heavy sauces and bread.

- Japanese sushi is based on rice—very often with sugar added to it. Try miso soup or any of the cooked meats and vegetables instead.

- Mexican food can be high in saturated fat and carbohydrates. Fajitas (1 tortilla) with the garnishes, grilled meats, and salads are fine. Avoid rice, refried beans, and nachos.

- Watch portion size when eating out. Many restaurant servings are large enough for two meals. The following guide will help you size up what you should be eating.

Sizing It Up*

1/2 cup fruit, vegetable, cooked cereal, pasta, or rice	a small fist
3 ounces cooked meat, poultry, or fish	a deck of cards
1/2 bagel	width of large coffee can lid
1 medium apple or orange	a baseball
1 1/2 ounces cheese	6 dice
1 tortilla	a small (7-inch) plate
1 muffin	a large egg
1 teaspoon butter	a thumb tip
2 tablespoons peanut butter	a golf ball

Food Insight News published by IFIC (International Food Information Council)

Quick Snacks

Snacks are important little meals that will help you through the day, especially during the first Quick Start phase. They can prevent that sinking feeling at 4 or 5 P.M. when your energy is low, or the mid-morning is-it-time-for-lunch clock watching.

Knowing what to snack on and how to have it handy can help prevent raids on the vending machine to satiate candy cravings.

Here are some ideas:

- The remainder of an extra large lunch salad, which you can take back to your office or home
- 1 ounce low-fat cheese (string cheese, stick cheese, small round individually packed wax-covered low-fat cheese)
- 1/4 cup low-fat cottage cheese
- 1 ounce nuts, such as almonds, pecans, or walnuts (1/4 cup). Keep small shelf-stable packages of nuts, the type that are found in the baking section of the supermarket, in your drawer at work, pocketbook, or briefcase. They're easy to carry around and contain portion-size amounts. Avoid salted, glazed, and oil-roasted nuts.

- 2 ounces deli meats, such as lean ham, turkey, chicken, or roast beef
- 1 hard-boiled egg. Keep a few hard-boiled eggs on hand for snacks. They will need to be refrigerated at the office.
- 1 ounce sunflower seeds
- 6 olives
- Any vegetables such as cucumber slices, celery sticks, broccoli or cauliflower florets, or bell pepper slices

stage I
quick start

This two-week meal plan is designed to start you off on cutting carbs from your meals.

When I give cooking classes and show these meals, the response always surprises me. "You mean I can eat all of that?" is the usual query. Knowing the quantities of each type of food you can eat will help you to build your own recipes to fit your lifestyle.

I have organized the menus into a meal-at-a-glance chart with some easy and quick meals midweek and those that take a little more time for the weekends. They are arranged to give variety throughout the day and over the days of the week.

Breakfast

There's plenty of variety in these breakfasts to fit all tastes, from Microwave Marinara Scramble to Southwestern Turkey Salsa Roll. Pick the ones you like and use them for this two-week period.

Mid-Morning Snack

When you first start reducing carbs, you will need to eat a mid-morning snack. I've included a section with some suggestions. (See pages 30–31.)

Lunch

There's a lunch for any occasion here—quick-take lunches that can be eaten at home or taken with you—more elaborate lunches for when you have more time or friends stop by.

Enjoy a Costa del Sol Tuna-Stuffed Tomatoes and Nutty Chicken Minestrone. These meals can be made at home and taken to work. They are commonly found on most lunch menus. If you are eating out, use these recipes as a guide for the portions you should eat.

I usually order my salads with the dressing on the side. Most salads come swimming in dressing. I find that 1 tablespoon of dressing gently coats the salad without overpowering it. So, I prefer to add the dressing to the salad myself. (See pages 28–29 for more tips on eating out.)

Mid-Afternoon Snack

When you first start reducing carbs, you will need to eat a mid-afternoon snack. (See pages 30–31.)

Dinner

Do you feel like Italian, French, or American food tonight? There's something from each ethnic group—

Tuscan Chicken and Tomato-Basil Relish with Toasted Almond Broccoli, Roasted Salmon and Herb Sauce with Braised Asparagus, and Chicken Burgers with Warm Mushroom Salad are some of the tempting meals.

For those days when you are really pressed for time, select Savory Sage Chicken with Italian Zucchini and Tomatoes or Jamaican Jerk Pork with Hearts of Palm Salad from Super Speed Suppers section of the book.

For weekends when you have more time and want something special, try the Dijon Chicken with Crunchy Couscous or Garlic-Stuffed Steak with Linguine and Asparagus from the Weekend Meals section of the book.

How low is low carb? It's important to reduce carbohydrate intake low enough for a period of time so that you eliminate the peaks of insulin secretion. Following the Quick Start 14 Day Meal Plan, you will consume an average of 35 to 45 grams of carbohydrates per day. Carbohydrate percentage is based on carbohydrates less fiber consumed, which is the normal way of calculating carbohydrate consumption. The balance of these meals is 11 percent of calories from carbs, 40 percent of calories from low-fat proteins, 36 percent of calories from monounsaturated fat, and 11 percent of calories from saturated fat.

To achieve the correct balance, I have structured the recipes as complete meals. Whatever meal you pick, it's best to stay with the entire menu given.

Quick Start 14-Day Menu Plan at a Glance

week 1	breakfast	lunch	dinner
sunday	Bacon and Cheese Egg Crepes 37	Sicilian Baked Mushrooms and Sausage 45	Dijon Chicken with Crunchy Couscous 147
monday	Microwave Eggs Parmesan 38	Chicken with Dilled Mustard 46	Greek Shrimp with Feta Cheese and Romaine with Fresh Cabbage Salad .131
tuesday	Mushroom, Turkey, and Tarragon Omelet 39	Quick-Take Cheese and Chicken Bundles 47	Hot Pepper Shrimp with Red Pepper and Endive Salad 53
wednesday	Southwestern Turkey Salsa Roll 40	Nutty Chicken Minestrone 48	Mediterranean Baked Fish with Zucchini Gratin and Green Salad 54
thursday	Microwave Marinara Scramble 41	Costa del Sol Tuna-Stuffed Tomatoes 49	Savory Sage Chicken with Italian Zucchini and Tomatoes 133
friday	Smoked Salmon-Stuffed Celery 42	Crunchy Asian Chicken Salad 50	Jamaican Jerk Pork with Hearts of Palm Salad .132
saturday	Sausage and Artichoke Frittata 43	Crab Gratin 51	Chicken Burgers with Warm Mushroom Salad 56

week 2	breakfast	lunch	dinner
sunday	Bacon and Cheese Egg Crepes 37	Sicilian Baked Mushrooms and Sausage 45	Garlic Stuffed-Steak with Linguine and Asparagus 148
monday	Microwave Eggs Parmesan 38	Chicken with Dilled Mustard 46	Crab Cakes with Slaw .57
tuesday	Mushroom, Turkey, and Tarragon Omelet 39	Quick-Take Cheese and Chicken Bundles 47	Sara Moulton's Pork Scallopini with Spinach and Mushrooms 58
wednesday	Southwestern Turkey Salsa Roll 40	Nutty Chicken Minestrone 48	Roasted Salmon and Herb Sauce with Braised Asparagus 59
thursday	Microwave Marinara Scramble 41	Costa del Sol Tuna-Stuffed Tomatoes 49	Tuscan Chicken with Tomato-Basil Relish and Toasted Almond Broccoli 60
friday	Smoked Salmon-Stuffed Celery 42	Crunchy Asian Chicken Salad 50	Savory Sage Chicken with Italian Zucchini and Tomatoes 133
saturday	Sausage and Artichoke Frittata 43	Crab Gratin 51	Veal Saltimbocca with Parmesan Zucchini and Italian Salad 150

quick start
breakfasts

Bacon and Cheese Egg Crepes

Making eggs into thin crepes is the secret to this dish. Be sure to use a good nonstick skillet for best results.

1 cup egg substitute
Freshly ground black pepper
Olive oil spray
6 ounces lean Canadian bacon, cut into 1-inch slices
¾ cup shredded part-skim milk mozzarella cheese
1 medium tomato, sliced

Preheat broiler. Mix egg substitute with pepper to taste. Heat a medium-size nonstick skillet on medium-high heat. Spray with olive oil spray and pour ½ cup egg substitute into a skillet and spread to make a thin layer. Let cook 2 minutes. Turn over, cook 1 minute. Remove from heat to a foil-lined baking sheet. Repeat with second half of egg mixture. Sprinkle bacon and cheese over crepes. Fold over once and place under broiler about 10 inches from heat. Broil 2 minutes or until cheese melts. Carefully slide onto a plate, place sliced tomatoes on the side and serve. Makes 2 servings.

Per serving: 335 calories, 43.2 grams protein, 7.0 grams carbohydrate, 14.2 grams fat (7.5 saturated), 73 milligrams cholesterol, 1227 milligrams sodium, 0 gram fiber

Helpful Hint

- *Make these crepes ahead, and fill and warm in a microwave oven when needed.*

Countdown

- *Preheat broiler.*
- *Make egg base.*
- *Complete recipe.*

Shopping List

Produce
1 medium tomato

Dairy
1 package shredded part-skim milk mozzarella cheese

Deli
6 ounces lean Canadian bacon

Staples
Egg substitute
Olive oil spray
Black peppercorns

Countdown

- *Make eggs.*
- *Arrange salad on 2 plates.*

Shopping List

Produce

1 medium tomato
1 small head romaine lettuce

Deli

¼ pound smoked turkey

Staples

Eggs (6 needed)
Parmesan cheese
Salt
Black peppercorns

Microwave Eggs Parmesan

Here is another quick microwave breakfast. ● *The timing of this dish depends on the power of your microwave oven. Also, some like their eggs dry, others wet. Select the timing according to your preference. Remember the eggs will continue to cook for about 1 minute after they are removed from the oven.*

4 egg whites
2 large eggs
¼ pound smoked turkey, cut into small cubes
2 tablespoons grated Parmesan cheese
Salt and freshly ground black pepper
Several romaine lettuce leaves
1 medium tomato, sliced

Place 2 egg whites and 1 whole egg in a microwave-safe bowl about 7 inches in diameter. Add 2 tablespoons turkey, 1 tablespoon Parmesan cheese, and salt and pepper to taste. Whisk with a fork. Microwave on high 1 minute. Stir and microwave 30 seconds and stir. For drier eggs, microwave 30 seconds more. Arrange lettuce leaves on 2 plates and place tomato slices on top. Spoon eggs onto plate. Using the same bowl, repeat for second serving. Makes 2 servings.

Per serving: 255 calories, 35.3 grams protein, 4.5 grams carbohydrate, 10.9 grams fat (4.0 saturated), 260 milligrams cholesterol, 394 milligrams sodium, 0.2 gram fiber

Mushroom, Turkey, and Tarragon Omelet

Omelets take only minutes to make. A perfect omelet is golden on the top with a delicate creamy center. The secret is to cook it over medium-high heat for only a couple of minutes.

4 egg whites

2 large whole eggs

¼ pound smoked turkey breast, cut into 1-inch cubes

1 teaspoon dried tarragon

Salt and freshly ground black pepper

Olive oil spray

1½ cups thinly sliced portobello mushrooms

1 medium tomato, cut into 1-inch pieces

Place eggs and egg whites in a bowl and stir in turkey, tarragon, and salt and pepper to taste. Heat a medium-size nonstick skillet over medium-high heat and spray with olive oil. Sauté mushrooms and tomatoes 2 minutes and remove. Pour in the egg mixture. Let the eggs set for about 30 seconds. Tip the pan and lightly move the eggs, cooking 1½ minutes until they all set. Cook a few seconds longer for firmer eggs.

Place the mushrooms and tomatoes on half the omelet and fold the omelet in half. Slide out of the pan by tipping the pan and holding a plate vertically against the side of the pan. Turn pan and plate to invert the omelet onto the plate. Cut in half and serve on 2 plates. Makes 2 servings.

Per serving: 228 calories, 31.5 grams protein, 4.7 grams carbohydrate, 9.3 grams fat (2.5 saturated), 253 milligrams cholesterol, 215 milligrams sodium, 0 gram fiber

Helpful Hints

- *Any herb can be used.*
- *Dried tarragon is called for in the recipe. If using dried herbs, make sure they are less than 6 months old.*
- *For best results, use a good-quality nonstick pan.*

Countdown

- *Prepare ingredients.*
- *Complete omelet.*

Shopping List

Produce

¼ pound portobello mushrooms

1 medium tomato

Deli

¼ pound smoked turkey breast

Staples

Eggs (6 needed)

Olive oil spray

Dried tarragon

Salt

Black peppercorns

Helpful Hints

- *Mexican-style, reduced-fat cheese can be used instead of Monterey Jack cheese.*
- *To help the morning rush, stuff the turkey the night before and warm just before eating.*

Countdown

- *Prepare ingredients.*
- *Complete dish.*

Shopping List

Dairy

1 small package shredded reduced-fat Monterey Jack or Mexican-style cheese

Deli

½ pound sliced, smoked turkey breast

Staples

1 small jar no-sugar-added tomato salsa

Southwestern Turkey Salsa Roll

Sliced turkey roll stuffed with Monterey Jack cheese and topped with salsa is a breakfast that can be made ahead and warmed in 1 minute in a microwave oven before eating.

½ pound sliced, smoked turkey breast

½ cup shredded reduced-fat Monterey Jack cheese

1 cup no-sugar-added tomato salsa

Place turkey slices on a counter or plate and sprinkle each slice with cheese. Roll up slices and divide between 2 plates. Microwave each plate on high for 1 minute or until cheese melts. If not using a microwave oven, place turkey rolls in a toaster oven or on a foil-lined tray under a broiler for 1 minute. Remove plates from microwave and spoon salsa over the top. Makes 2 servings.

Per serving: 310 calories, 44.0 grams protein, 10.4 grams carbohydrate, 8.5 grams fat (4.2 saturated), 90 milligrams cholesterol, 1036 milligrams sodium, 4.0 grams fiber

Microwave Marinara Scramble

This breakfast takes just minutes to make in a microwave oven. A rich, thick marinara sauce gives these scrambled eggs a taste of Naples. ● The timing of this dish depends on the power of your microwave oven. Also, some like their eggs dry, others wet. Select the timing according to your preference. Remember the eggs will continue to cook for about 1 minute after they are removed from the oven.

5 ounces washed, ready-to-eat baby spinach (4 cups)

¼ pound lean ham, cut into 1-inch pieces

1 cup egg substitute

¼ cup low-salt, no-sugar-added marinara sauce

Salt and freshly ground black pepper

6 tablespoons shredded part-skim milk mozzarella cheese

Place spinach and ham in a microwave-safe bowl and microwave on high for 2 minutes. Divide between 2 plates.

Combine egg substitute and marinara sauce together in a microwave-safe bowl. Season with salt and pepper to taste. Cover with plastic wrap or a plate. Microwave on high for 4 minutes. Stir and divide in half. Place each portion on top of spinach and ham. Sprinkle 2 tablespoons mozzarella cheese on top of each portion. Makes 2 servings.

Per serving: 250 calories, 33.6 grams protein, 10.6 grams carbohydrate, 8.6 grams fat (4.0 saturated), 43 milligrams cholesterol, 1127 milligrams sodium, 3.6 grams fiber

Helpful Hints

● If you don't have a microwave oven, sauté the spinach for 1 minute in a small skillet and remove to a plate. Scramble the eggs in the same skillet.

● If baby spinach is unavailable, use any type of spinach or lettuce.

Countdown

● Microwave spinach.
● Microwave scrambled eggs.

Shopping List

Produce
1 bag washed, ready-to-eat baby spinach (5 ounces needed)

Dairy
1 small package shredded part-skim milk mozzarella cheese

Deli
¼ pound lean ham

Grocery
1 small container low-salt, no-sugar-added marinara sauce

Staples
Egg substitute (8 ounces needed)
Salt
Black peppercorns

Helpful Hints

- *A quick way to cut chives is to snip them with a scissors.*
- *Freeze-dried chives can be used instead of fresh.*

Countdown

- *Prepare ingredients.*
- *Assemble dish.*

Shopping List

Produce
  1 small bunch chives

Dairy
  1 small carton sour cream

Seafood
  ¾ pound smoked salmon

Staples
  Celery
  Black peppercorns

Smoked Salmon-Stuffed Celery

If you're in a hurry, make this breakfast the night before and take it with you to eat on the run.

¾ pound smoked salmon
¼ cup sour cream
2 tablespoons snipped chives
Freshly ground black pepper
8 medium celery stalks

Chop salmon. This can be done in a food processor or by hand. Mix with sour cream and chives. Add black pepper to taste. Spread into celery and cut stalks into 2-inch pieces. Divide between 2 plates. Makes 2 servings.

Per serving: 290 calories, 33.4 grams protein, 13.2 grams carbohydrate, 13.9 grams fat (4.9 saturated), 53 milligrams cholesterol, 1625 milligrams sodium, 4.0 grams fiber

Sausage and Artichoke Frittata

Plump, juicy frittatas take about 15 minutes to make. They can be made ahead and eaten at room temperature or reheated in a microwave oven. They differ from omelets. An omelet is cooked fast over high, heat making it creamy and runny, while a frittata is cooked slowly over low heat, making it firm and set. A frittata needs to be cooked on both sides. Some people flip it in the pan. A much easier way is to place it in a preheated oven to finish cooking or under the broiler for half a minute. ● *There are several types of low-fat turkey sausages available in the supermarkets. They range from mild to spicy hot. Choose whichever type fits your palate.*

2 teaspoons olive oil
2 low-fat turkey sausages, cut into ½-inch slices (6 ounces)
4 egg whites
2 large whole eggs
¾ cup drained marinated artichoke hearts, cut in half
1 tablespoon freeze-dried chives
Salt and freshly ground black pepper

Preheat oven to 400 degrees. Heat olive oil in a 7- to 8-inch nonstick skillet on medium-high heat. Sauté sausage 3 minutes. Mix egg whites, whole eggs, and artichokes together. Add chives and salt and pepper to taste. Reduce heat to medium and pour egg mixture into skillet. Spread to cover sausage and artichokes. Leave to set on the bottom for 3 minutes. Place in oven for 7 minutes or until eggs set. If you like drier eggs, leave for 1 further minute. Makes 2 servings.

Per serving: 337 calories, 29.0 grams protein, 7.0 grams carbohydrate, 21.3 grams fat (4.2 saturated), 258 milligrams cholesterol, 893 milligrams sodium, 1.0 gram fiber

Helpful Hint

● *Egg substitute can be used instead of 4 egg whites and 2 whole eggs.*

Countdown

● *Preheat oven to 400 degrees.*
● *Prepare ingredients.*
● *Make frittata.*

Shopping List

Meat
   1 small package low-fat turkey sausages (6 ounces needed)

Grocery
   1 small jar/can marinated artichoke hearts
   1 small container freeze-dried chives

Staples
   Eggs (6 needed)
   Olive oil
   Salt
   Black peppercorns

quick start
lunches

Sicilian Baked Mushrooms and Sausage

Mushrooms baked with garlic and sausage and topped with cheese and breadcrumbs is a dish that originates from Palermo in Sicily. The dish can be baked in an oven or takes only minutes in a microwave oven.

Olive oil spray

¾ pound low-fat turkey sausage, cut into 1-inch pieces

3¾ cups thinly sliced button mushrooms

4 garlic cloves, crushed

⅛ teaspoon crushed red pepper flakes

Salt and freshly ground black pepper

¼ cup chopped fresh parsley

2 tablespoons breadcrumbs

3 tablespoons grated Parmesan cheese

Spray a 10-inch microwave-safe pie plate with olive oil spray. Add the sausages and microwave on high for 2 minutes. Remove from microwave and pour off fat. Add mushrooms, garlic, and red pepper. Add salt and pepper to taste. Sprinkle parsley over mushrooms. Sprinkle breadcrumbs and Parmesan cheese on top. Microwave on high for 5 minutes. Or place in a preheated 400-degree oven for 15 minutes. Divide between 2 plates. Makes 2 servings.

Per serving: 388 calories, 33.7 grams protein, 11.2 grams carbohydrate, 21.5 grams fat (7.0 saturated), 94 milligrams cholesterol, 1273 milligrams sodium, 0 gram fiber

Helpful Hints

- *Any combination of mushrooms can be used.*
- *Buy sliced mushrooms or slice them in a food processor.*
- *Crushed red pepper can be found in the spice section of the supermarket.*
- *Buy good-quality Parmesan cheese and ask the market to grate it for you or chop it in your food processor. Freeze extra for quick use. You can quickly spoon out what you need and leave the rest frozen.*

Countdown

- *If using an oven, preheat to 400 degrees.*
- *Prepare ingredients.*
- *Make mushrooms.*

Shopping List

Produce
  10 ounces button mushrooms, sliced
  1 small bunch fresh parsley

Meat
  ¾ pound low-fat turkey sausage

Grocery
  1 small jar crushed red pepper flakes
  1 small container plain breadcrumbs

Staples
  Olive oil spray
  Parmesan cheese
  Garlic
  Salt
  Black peppercorns

Helpful Hint

- *Dried dill is called for in the recipe. If using dried herbs, make sure they are less than 6 months old.*

Countdown

- *Prepare ingredients.*
- *Complete dish.*

Shopping List

Deli

3/4 pound thick-sliced (about 1/4 inch) deli chicken breast

Staples

Celery (12 stalks needed)
Dijon mustard
Dried dill
Mayonnaise

Chicken with Dilled Mustard

This lunch of sliced chicken breast topped with a dill mustard sauce and crunchy sliced celery requires no cooking and can be assembled the night before. It's also a good recipe for leftover chicken.

3/4 pound thick-sliced (about 1/4 inch) deli chicken breast
3 tablespoons Dijon mustard
1 1/2 tablespoons mayonnaise
1 1/2 teaspoons dried dill
12 medium celery stalks, thinly sliced (6 cups)

Divide chicken between 2 plates. Mix mustard, mayonnaise, and dill together and spread half the mixture over the chicken. Place celery slices on top and spread remaining sauce on top. Makes 2 servings.

Per serving: 440 calories, 57.9 grams protein, 19.4 grams carbohydrate, 18.5 grams fat (2.9 saturated), 148 milligrams cholesterol, 1146 milligrams sodium, 6.0 grams fiber

Quick-Take Cheese and Chicken Bundles

Roasted chicken, blue cheese, walnuts, and yogurt blend together to make a tasty spread that is rolled into lettuce leaves. These little bundles can be made ahead and taken to eat on the run.

2 ounces crumbled blue cheese (½ cup)

¼ cup plain nonfat yogurt

2 tablespoons broken walnuts

½ pound roasted chicken strips

Several romaine lettuce leaves (about 6)

4 medium celery stalks

Place blue cheese, yogurt, walnuts, and chicken in the bowl of a food processor fitted with a chopping blade. Process to a spreadable consistency. Place lettuce leaves on a countertop and spread chicken mixture on leaves. Roll up lengthwise and wrap in aluminum foil or parchment paper. Cut celery stalks into 2-inch pieces and serve on the side.
Makes 2 servings.

Per serving: 411 calories, 46.9 grams protein, 13.3 grams carbohydrate, 21.3 grams fat (7.2 saturated), 118 milligrams cholesterol, 652 milligrams sodium, 3.2 grams fiber

Helpful Hints

- *Any large lettuce leaves can be used.*
- *Crumbled blue cheese can be found in the dairy case of most supermarkets.*
- *Buy plain or original flavor roasted chicken strips. Stay away from honey roasted or barbecue chicken.*

Countdown

- *Prepare ingredients.*
- *Make bundles.*

Shopping List

Produce
1 small head romaine lettuce

Dairy
1 small carton plain nonfat yogurt
1 small package crumbled blue cheese

Meat
1 package roasted chicken strips (½ pound needed)

Grocery
1 small package broken walnut pieces

Staples
Celery

Helpful Hints

- *Walnuts, pecans, or almonds can be substituted for pistachio nuts.*
- *Buy good-quality Parmesan cheese and ask the market to grate it for you or chop it in your food processor. Freeze extra for quick use. You can quickly spoon out what you need and leave the rest frozen.*
- *Shredded carrots are available in the produce section of the market.*

Countdown

- *Prepare ingredients.*
- *Make soup.*

Shopping List

Produce
1 small package shredded carrots
1 bag washed, ready-to-eat spinach
1 medium tomato
1 small bunch basil

Meat
½ pound roasted chicken strips or pieces

Grocery
1 small package shelled pistachio nuts

Staples
Olive Oil
Parmesan cheese
Fat-free, low-sodium chicken broth (12 ounces needed)
Celery
Salt
Black peppercorns

Nutty Chicken Minestrone

This minestrone is a refreshing blend of flavors using fresh vegetables, chicken, and pistachio nuts combined with the perfume of fresh basil. Minestra is Italian for soup. Minestrone is a thick soup that can be made in 20 minutes using store-bought cooked chicken breasts. Leftover chicken can be used for this recipe. ● *Look for shelled pistachio nuts. They are now available in most supermarkets.*

2 teaspoons olive oil
¼ cup shredded carrots
¼ cup sliced celery
1 medium tomato, diced (1 cup)
1½ cups fat-free, low-sodium chicken broth
1½ cups water
½ pound roasted, ready-to-eat chicken strips
Salt and freshly ground black pepper
¼ pound washed, ready-to-eat spinach (1 cup)
¼ cup fresh basil
2 tablespoons freshly grated Parmesan cheese
2 tablespoons coarsely chopped pistachio nuts

Heat the oil in a large saucepan on medium-high heat. Add the carrot and celery. Sauté for 5 minutes. Do not brown the vegetables. Stir the vegetables gently, being careful not to break them up.

Add the tomato, chicken broth, and water. The liquid should cover the vegetables. Add more water, if needed. Bring to a simmer and partially cover with a lid, leaving space for steam to escape. Simmer for 10 minutes. Add the chicken and simmer 5 more minutes. Add salt and pepper to taste. Remove from heat. Stir in the spinach and basil. Let stand 1 minute. Spoon into 2 soup bowls. Sprinkle each bowl with Parmesan cheese and pistachio nuts.
Makes 2 servings.

Per serving: 379 calories, 46.6 grams protein, 10.1 grams carbohydrate, 18.4 grams fat (4.3 saturated), 103 milligrams cholesterol, 731 milligrams sodium, 1.3 grams fiber

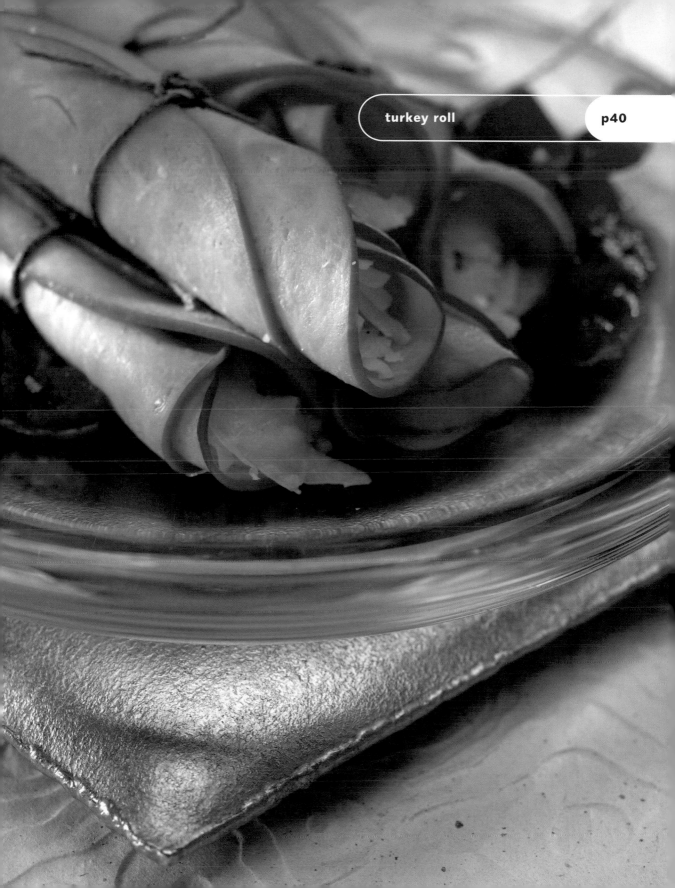

turkey roll **p40**

p58

sara moulton's pork
scaloppine

Costa del Sol Tuna–Stuffed Tomatoes

Olives, pimientos, and almonds mix with tuna to make a Spanish tuna salad. This is also a good recipe for leftover chicken or other seafood.

2 large tomatoes
2 tablespoons mayonnaise
Freshly ground black pepper
9 ounces canned white tuna
    packed in water, drained
6 pitted green olives, sliced
1 cup sliced sweet pimiento,
    drained
2½ tablespoons slivered almonds
    (1 ounce)
Several lettuce leaves, washed
    and torn into bite-size pieces

Cut tomatoes in half, scoop out pulp and seeds, and take a thin slice off the rounded bottom of each half. This will help the tomatoes sit straight on the plate. Set the tomato halves aside. Mix mayonnaise with black pepper to taste. Add the tuna, olives, pimiento, and almonds. Mix to combine. Taste for seasoning and add more, if necessary.

Place the lettuce on 2 plates and the tomato halves on the lettuce. Fill the tomatoes with the tuna salad. Serve extra salad on the lettuce. Makes 2 servings.

Per serving: 404 calories, 39.2 grams protein, 12.6 grams carbohydrate, 22.5 grams fat (2.3 saturated), 61 milligrams cholesterol, 945 milligrams sodium, 0.2 gram fiber

Helpful Hints

- Use good-quality, water-packed, canned tuna.
- To help the tomato halves sit straight, cut a thin slice from the rounded ends.
- Any type of lettuce can be used.

Countdown

- Prepare ingredients.
- Make recipe.

Shopping List

Produce
2 large tomatoes
1 small head lettuce

Grocery
9 ounces canned white tuna packed in water
1 container pitted green olives (6 needed)
1 jar/can sweet pimientos (1 cup needed)
1 small package slivered almonds (1 ounce needed)

Staples
Mayonnaise
Black peppercorns

Helpful Hint
- Any type of lettuce can be used.

Countdown
- Prepare ingredients.
- Assemble salad.

Shopping List

Produce
1 package washed, ready-to-eat mesclun or field greens
1 small bunch scallions

Meat
½ pound roasted, ready-to-eat chicken pieces

Grocery
1 small can sliced water chestnuts
1 jar ground ginger

Staples
No-sugar-added oil (olive or canola) and vinegar dressing
Low-sodium soy sauce

Crunchy Asian Chicken Salad

Roasted or rotisserie chicken takes on a new dimension in this quick salad. Adding ginger and soy sauce to a bottled oil and vinegar dressing gives it an Asian flavor. A mixture of baby or very young greens is called mesclun or sometimes field greens.

½ pound roasted, ready-to-eat chicken pieces

1 cup drained, sliced water chestnuts

4 scallions, sliced (½ cup)

3 tablespoons no-sugar-added oil (olive or canola) and vinegar dressing

2 teaspoons low-sodium soy sauce

½ teaspoon ground ginger

4 cups washed, ready-to-eat mesclun

Place chicken pieces, water chestnuts, and scallions in a large bowl. Mix dressing, soy sauce, and ginger together and pour over chicken. Toss well. Divide mesclun between 2 plates and spoon chicken salad on top. Makes 2 servings.

Per serving: 378 calories, 38.7 grams protein, 17.3 grams carbohydrate, 18.1 grams fat (3.1 saturated), 96 milligrams cholesterol, 437 milligrams sodium, 4.6 grams fiber

Crab Gratin

Good-quality crabmeat is the secret to this quick lunch. Fresh crabmeat from the seafood case would be best; but if this is difficult to find, use pasteurized crabmeat.

3 tablespoons mayonnaise

2 tablespoons lemon juice or water

¾ pound lump crabmeat (about 2½ cups)

Salt and freshly ground black pepper

2 large tomatoes, stem removed, cut into ½-inch slices

¼ cup shredded reduced-fat Cheddar cheese

Preheat broiler. Mix mayonnaise and lemon juice together in a small bowl. Add crabmeat and flake with a fork as it's mixed with the mayonnaise. Add salt and pepper to taste. Place tomato slices on foil-lined baking tray. Spoon crab over tomatoes and sprinkle cheese on top. Place under broiler 2 to 3 minutes or until cheese melts. Remove to 2 plates and serve. Makes 2 servings.

Per serving: 382 calories, 37.1 grams protein, 9.1 grams carbohydrate, 21.2 grams fat (4.5 saturated), 149 milligrams cholesterol, 746 milligrams sodium, 0 gram fiber

Helpful Hints

- *Frozen crab can be used. The flavor will be fine; the crabmeat will be soft.*
- *Pasteurized crabmeat can be found in the refrigerated section of the seafood department.*

Countdown

- *Preheat broiler.*
- *Prepare ingredients.*
- *Make gratin.*

Shopping List

Produce

2 large tomatoes

Dairy

1 small package shredded reduced-fat Cheddar cheese

Seafood

¾ pound lump crabmeat

Staples

Lemon

Mayonnaise

Salt

Black peppercorns

quick start
dinners

Hot Pepper Shrimp with Red Bell Pepper and Endive Salad

Hot, spicy shrimp with lots of garlic is a popular Spanish tapas dish. The shrimp dish is normally served on its own for tapas; but by adding a quick salad, it becomes an entire meal.
● *Belgian endive, sometimes called chicory, is a small cigar-shaped head of lettuce that is creamy white. It has tightly packed leaves and can be cleaned by wiping the outer leaves with a damp paper towel. The leaves will turn brown if soaked in water.*

Hot Pepper Shrimp

10 ounces washed, ready-to-eat spinach (about 8 cups)

6 garlic cloves, crushed (divided use)

Salt and freshly ground black pepper

1 tablespoon olive oil

Pinch of crushed red pepper flakes

¾ pound shrimp, peeled

2 tablespoons chopped fresh parsley

Place spinach and 3 crushed garlic cloves in a large microwave-safe bowl. Microwave on high for 3 minutes. Add salt and pepper to taste. Toss well. Divide between 2 plates. Heat a medium-size nonstick skillet on medium-high heat. Add olive oil and red pepper flakes. When oil is hot, add shrimp and remaining 3 crushed garlic cloves. Toss shrimp in oil for 2 to 3 minutes or until shrimp are no longer translucent. Remove from heat and sprinkle with parsley and salt and pepper to taste. Spoon over spinach including pan juices. Makes 2 servings.

Per serving: 299 calories, 41.4 grams protein, 11.5 grams carbohydrate, 10.7 grams fat (1.5 saturated), 260 milligrams cholesterol, 426 milligrams sodium, 7.2 grams fiber

Red Bell Pepper and Endive Salad

2 medium heads Belgian endive lettuce, sliced (2 cups)

1 medium red bell pepper, sliced in 1-inch strips (2 cups)

2 tablespoons no-sugar-added oil (olive or canola) and vinegar dressing

Salt and freshly ground black pepper

Wipe endive with a damp paper towel. Cut off about ½ inch from the bottom or flat end and discard. Cut endive into ½-inch slices and place in a small bowl. Add red pepper strips to bowl. Drizzle with dressing and add salt and pepper to taste. Toss well. Makes 2 servings.

Per serving: 253 calories, 1.3 grams protein, 7.1 grams carbohydrate, 25.2 grams fat (4.4 saturated), 0 milligram cholesterol, 239 milligrams sodium, 0 gram fiber

Helpful Hints

● *Shelled shrimp is available at most supermarket seafood counters. The slightly higher cost is worth the time saved.*
● *A quick way to chop parsley is to wash, dry, and snip the leaves right off the stem with a scissors.*
● *Any type of lettuce can be used for the salad.*

Countdown

● *Make salad.*
● *Prepare shrimp.*

Shopping List

Produce

1 (10-ounce) bag washed, ready-to-eat spinach

1 medium red bell pepper (2 cups sliced)

1 small bunch parsley (2 tablespoons used)

2 medium heads Belgian endive lettuce

Seafood

¾ pound shelled shrimp

Grocery

1 small bottle crushed red pepper flakes

Staples

Olive oil

Garlic

No-sugar-added oil (olive or canola) and vinegar dressing

Salt

Black peppercorns

Mediterranean Baked Fish with Zucchini Gratin and Green Salad

Try a taste of the Mediterranean with this baked snapper topped with pine nuts, olives, and pimiento. An Italian friend makes the best zucchini with a hint of melted cheese on top. She told me her secret: Grate the zucchini using a grater with large holes. It cooks faster and tastes better. I created this quick Zucchini Gratin with memories of her wonderful dish.

Mediterranean Baked Fish

3/4 pound grouper fillets
Salt and freshly ground black pepper
2 teaspoons olive oil
2 tablespoons pine nuts
6 pitted green olives, cut in half
1/2 cup drained, sliced sweet pimiento

Preheat oven to 400 degrees. Line a baking sheet with aluminum foil. Rinse grouper and pat dry with paper towel. Sprinkle fish with salt and pepper to taste. Place on prepared baking sheet and drizzle oil on top. Bake 10 minutes. Spoon pine nuts, olives, and pimiento over fish. Return to oven for 10 minutes. Makes 2 servings.

Per serving: 255 calories, 33.2 grams protein, 2.2 grams carbohydrate, 8.0 grams fat (1.2 saturated), 62 milligrams cholesterol, 373 milligrams sodium, 0 gram fiber

Zucchini Gratin

1 pound zucchini, grated (3 1/2 to 4 cups)
2 tablespoons grated Parmesan cheese
Salt and freshly ground black pepper
2 teaspoons olive oil

Place zucchini in a microwave-safe bowl. Microwave on high for 2 minutes. If you do not have a microwave oven, bring a small saucepan of water to a boil and add zucchini. Drain as soon as the water comes back to a boil. Spoon half the zucchini into a shallow ovenproof dish. Sprinkle 1 tablespoon Parmesan cheese and salt and pepper to taste. Cover with remaining zucchini and finish with Parmesan cheese and salt and pepper to taste. Drizzle olive oil on top. Place in same oven with fish for 5 minutes or until cheese melts. Makes 2 servings.

Per serving: 129 calories, 7.9 grams protein, 8.0 grams carbohydrate, 8.4 grams fat (2.8 saturated), 9 milligrams cholesterol, 219 milligrams sodium,1.2 grams fiber

Helpful Hints
- Any type of mild white fish fillet can be used in this recipe. Bake about 10 minutes per inch of thickness.
- Grate the zucchini in a food processor using a julienne cutting blade or use a grater with 1/4-inch holes.

Countdown
- Preheat oven to 400 degrees.
- Make fish.
- While fish bakes, make zucchini.
- Assemble salad.

continues

Green Salad

*4 cups washed, ready-to-eat
lettuce*

*2 tablespoons no-sugar-added oil
(olive or canola) and vinegar
dressing*

Place lettuce in a large bowl and toss with
dressing. Makes 2 servings.

Per serving: 84 calories, 0.6 grams protein,
1.9 grams carbohydrate, 8.5 grams fat (1.3 saturated),
0 milligrams cholesterol, 81 milligrams sodium,
0.3 grams fiber

Shopping List

Produce

1 pound zucchini

*1 bag washed, ready-to-eat
lettuce*

Seafood

³/₄ pound grouper fillets

Grocery

*1 small package pine nuts
(¹/₂ ounce needed)*

*1 small container pitted green
olives*

*1 small jar/can sweet
pimientos (¹/₂ cup used)*

Staples

Olive oil

*No-sugar-added oil (olive or
canola) and vinegar dressing*

Parmesan cheese

Salt

Black peppercorns

Chicken Burgers with Warm Mushroom Salad

Helpful Hints

- Parsley or cilantro can be used instead of basil in the chicken recipe.
- Only 2 tablespoons pesto are needed for the burgers. Extra pesto sauce can be frozen for another time.
- To save washing a second skillet, cook the mushrooms first, then remove and use the same skillet for the burgers.
- A quick way to chop basil is to wash, dry, and snip the leaves right off the stem with a scissors.

Countdown

- Sauté mushrooms and remove from skillet.
- Prepare chicken burgers while mushrooms cook.
- Prepare tomato topping for chicken.
- Cook chicken burgers.

Shopping List

Produce
1 medium tomato
1 small bunch fresh basil
1 small bunch scallions
½ pound portobello mushrooms
1 small head radicchio

Meat
¾ pound ground white-meat chicken

Grocery
1 small container prepared pesto sauce

Staples
Olive oil spray
Garlic
No-sugar-added oil (olive or canola) and vinegar dressing
Salt
Black peppercorns

These burgers are tasty and juicy and take only a few minutes to make. Ground white-meat chicken is the key here. Make sure the package says "ground white-meat chicken." If the package says "ground chicken," then skin, fat, and other parts of the chicken can be used. Prepared pesto sauce gives these burgers a taste of Italy and keeps the meat juicy.

Chicken Burgers

¾ pound ground white-meat chicken
2 tablespoons prepared pesto sauce
½ teaspoon freshly ground black pepper
Dash of salt
Olive oil spray
1 medium tomato, coarsely chopped
Several basil leaves, cut into bite-size pieces
1 scallion, sliced
Salt and freshly ground black pepper

Mix chicken, pesto, black pepper, and salt together in a small bowl. Shape into burgers about 3½- to 4-inches in diameter and ½ inch thick. Heat a medium-size nonstick skillet on medium-high heat. Spray with olive oil spray and sauté burgers 5 minutes on each side. Remove to 2 dinner plates.

Toss tomato, basil, and scallion together, and add salt and pepper to taste. Spoon over cooked burgers. Makes 2 servings.

Per serving: 381 calories, 56.6 grams protein, 7.0 grams carbohydrate, 15.0 grams fat (3.9 saturated), 149 milligrams cholesterol, 410 milligrams sodium, 0.8 gram fiber

Warm Mushroom Salad

Olive oil spray
½ pound sliced portobello mushrooms (about 3 cups)
2 garlic cloves, crushed
Salt and freshly ground black pepper
2 tablespoons no-sugar-added oil (olive or canola) and vinegar dressing
Several radicchio leaves

Heat a nonstick skillet on medium-high heat and spray with olive oil. Add mushrooms and garlic. Sauté 5 minutes. Add salt and pepper to taste. Remove to a small bowl. Add dressing and toss well. Place radicchio leaves on 2 dinner plates. Spoon mushrooms onto leaves. Makes 2 servings.

Per serving: 127 calories, 1.9 grams protein, 5.4 grams carbohydrate, 10.2 grams fat (1.6 saturated), 0 milligram cholesterol, 80 milligrams sodium, 0.2 gram fiber

Crab Cakes and Slaw

Crab cakes are very popular. Nearly every restaurant seems to have its own version, but the base usually has Worcestershire sauce, hot pepper sauce, and onions or scallions. Fresh crabmeat is best for this recipe. If difficult to find, use pasteurized crabmeat. ● Homemade coleslaw is a breeze with a ready-to-eat, sliced coleslaw mix from the produce department.

Crab Cakes

1 pound fresh or pasteurized crabmeat (2½ cups)

2 tablespoons reduced-fat mayonnaise

2 tablespoons Worcestershire sauce

Several drops hot pepper sauce

4 scallions, sliced (½ cup)

2 tablespoons Dijon mustard

2 egg whites

3 tablespoons plain breadcrumbs

Salt and freshly ground black pepper

2 tablespoons olive oil

Drain crabmeat. Flake meat with a fork while looking for any shell or cartilage that might remain. Mix the mayonnaise, Worcestershire sauce, hot pepper sauce, scallions, mustard, egg whites, and breadcrumbs together in a medium-size bowl. Add salt and pepper to taste. Stir in crabmeat. Shape into 6 cakes about 3 inches in diameter. Heat olive oil in a medium-size nonstick skillet on medium heat. Add crab cakes and cook 5 minutes. Do not move crab cakes during this time. Carefully turn and cook 5 minutes. Serve crab cakes with coleslaw. Makes 2 servings.

Per serving: 435 calories, 46.0 grams protein, 5.5 grams carbohydrate, 22.0 grams fat (3.4 saturated), 182 milligrams cholesterol, 1572 milligrams sodium, 0 gram fiber

Slaw

2 tablespoons reduced-fat mayonnaise

¼ cup distilled white vinegar

Sugar substitute equivalent to 2 teaspoons sugar

Salt and freshly ground black pepper

4 cups ready-to-eat coleslaw mix

Mix mayonnaise, vinegar, and sugar substitute together in a medium-size bowl. Add salt and pepper to taste. Add coleslaw mix and toss well. Add more salt and pepper, if needed. Place on 2 plates. Makes 2 servings.

Per serving: 94 calories, 2.0 grams protein, 11.1 grams carbohydrate, 5.4 grams fat (1.0 saturated), 5 milligrams cholesterol, 139 milligrams sodium, 2.0 grams fiber

Helpful Hints

● Frozen crabmeat can be used. The flavor will be fine; the texture will be softer than fresh crabmeat.

● Pasteurized crabmeat can be found in the refrigerated section of the seafood department.

● Bags with different types of cabbage slaw, cut and ready to use, can be found in the produce section of the supermarket. Use whichever you like.

Countdown

● Make slaw.

● Make crab cakes.

Shopping List

Produce

1 package ready-to-eat coleslaw mix

1 small bunch scallions

Seafood

1 pound fresh or pasteurized crabmeat

Grocery

1 small container plain breadcrumbs (3 tablespoons used)

Staples

Reduced-fat mayonnaise

Worcestershire sauce

Hot pepper sauce

Dijon mustard

Eggs (2 needed)

Olive oil

Distilled white vinegar

Sugar substitute

Salt

Black peppercorns

Helpful Hints

- *Any type of green vegetable can be substituted for spinach.*
- *Look for shelled pistachio nuts in the supermarket.*

Countdown

- *Preheat oven to 400 degrees.*
- *Make spinach and mushrooms.*
- *Make pork scallopini.*

Shopping List

Produce

2 medium tomatoes

1 (10-ounce) bag washed, ready-to-eat spinach

¾ pound sliced portobello mushrooms

Meat

¾ pound pork tenderloin

Grocery

1 small package shelled pistachio nuts

Staples

Olive oil

Garlic

Salt

Black peppercorns

Sara Moulton's Pork Scallopini with Spinach and Mushrooms

"Pork Scallopini with fresh sautéed tomatoes and garlic," was the instant answer TV chef Sara Moulton gave me when I asked her what she serves her family for a quick meal.

Sara Moulton's Pork Scallopini

¾ pound pork tenderloin

2 tablespoons finely chopped pistachio nuts

Salt and freshly ground black pepper

1 teaspoon olive oil

2 medium garlic cloves, crushed

2 medium tomatoes, cut into 1-inch pieces (2 cups)

Remove fat from pork and cut into 1-inch slices. Place slices between 2 pieces of plastic wrap and flatten with the bottom of a heavy pan or meat bat. Place pistachio nuts on a plate and season with salt and pepper to taste. Press into pork on both sides. Heat oil in a large nonstick skillet on medium-high heat. Brown pork 1 minute, then turn and brown second side 1 minute. Salt and pepper the cooked sides. Remove to a plate. Add garlic and tomatoes to the skillet and cook 3 minutes. Spoon tomatoes over pork and serve. Makes 2 servings.

Per serving: 398 calories, 53.9 grams protein, 8.8 grams carbohydrate, 16.0 grams fat (3.9 saturated), 159 milligrams cholesterol, 126 milligrams sodium, 0 gram fiber

Spinach and Mushrooms

10 ounces washed, ready-to-eat spinach (about 8 cups)

¾ pound portobello mushrooms, sliced (4½ cups)

2 teaspoons olive oil

Salt and freshly ground black pepper

Place spinach and mushrooms in a large microwave-safe bowl. Microwave on high 5 minutes. Remove and toss well. Add olive oil and salt and pepper to taste. Toss again. Makes 2 servings.

Per serving: 126 calories, 7.8 grams protein, 11.2 grams carbohydrate, 6.2 grams fat (0.6 saturated), 0 milligram cholesterol, 174 milligrams sodium, 7.2 grams fiber

Roasted Salmon and Herb Sauce with Braised Asparagus

Salmon, sprayed with a little olive oil and sprinkled with salt and pepper, takes on a buttery, creamy texture when roasted in a 350 degree oven for 20 minutes. It is served with an herb sauce that takes only minutes in a food processor.

Roast Salmon and Herb Sauce

2 (6-ounce) salmon fillets
Olive oil spray
Salt and freshly ground black pepper
1 packed cup arugula
1/4 cup plain nonfat yogurt, drained
2 teaspoons fresh lemon or lime juice
1 tablespoon mayonnaise
1 medium tomato, sliced

Preheat oven to 350 degrees. Line a baking sheet with aluminum foil, spray both sides of the fillet with olive oil spray, and place salmon on the sheet. Sprinkle with salt and pepper to taste. Roast in oven 20 minutes.

Meanwhile, remove any large stems from arugula and place in a food processor. Add yogurt, lemon juice, and mayonnaise. Process until smooth. Add salt and pepper to taste. Spoon over roasted salmon. Place sliced tomatoes on the side. Makes 2 servings.

> Per serving: 375 calories, 44.8 grams protein, 6.8 grams carbohydrate, 16.6 grams fat (3.5 saturated), 123 milligrams cholesterol, 180 milligrams sodium, 0 gram fiber

Braised Asparagus

3/4 pound asparagus
1/2 cup water
1 teaspoon olive oil
Salt and freshly ground black pepper

Wash asparagus and cut about 1 inch off the woody ends. Place in a large nonstick skillet just large enough to hold them in one layer. Add the water, olive oil, and salt and pepper to taste. Bring to a simmer on medium-high heat and cover with lid. Lower heat to medium-low and cook 10 minutes. Check the water halfway through the cooking and add more if the pan is dry. Serve with the salmon. Makes 2 servings.

> Per serving: 43 calories, 3 grams protein, 4.5 grams carbohydrate, 206 grams fat (0.4 saturated), 0 milligram cholesterol, 138 milligrams sodium, 3.6 grams fiber

Helpful Hints

- *If you do not have a food processor, cut the arugula into small strips and mix with the other ingredients.*
- *If using thin asparagus, cut the braising time in half.*

Countdown

- *Preheat oven to 350 degrees.*
- *Place salmon in oven.*
- *Make asparagus.*
- *While salmon and asparagus cook, make herb sauce.*

Shopping List

Produce
3/4 pound asparagus
1 bunch arugula (1 1/2 ounces needed)
1 medium tomato

Dairy
1 small carton plain nonfat yogurt (2 ounces needed)

Seafood
2 (6-ounce) salmon fillets

Staples
Olive oil
Olive oil spray
Lemon or lime
Mayonnaise
Salt
Black peppercorns

Tuscan Chicken with Tomato-Basil Relish and Toasted Almond Broccoli

Helpful Hints

- Any type of ripe tomato can be used for the relish.
- Fresh parsley or cilantro can be used instead of basil.
- A quick way to chop basil is to wash, dry, and snip the leaves right off the stem with a scissors.
- To save washing an extra skillet, sauté the almonds for a few minutes in a large skillet, then remove them and use the same skillet to cook the chicken.

Countdown

- Make tomato relish.
- Sauté almonds.
- Prepare chicken.
- Make broccoli.

Shopping List

Produce

1 large plum tomato
1 small bunch basil
1/2 pound broccoli florets

Meat

3/4 pound boneless, skinless chicken breasts

Grocery

1 small jar sliced, sweet pimientos
1 1/2 ounces sliced almonds

Staples

Red onion
Olive oil spray
Olive oil
Balsamic vinegar
Salt
Black peppercorns

A fresh tomato-basil relish tops this simple chicken dish. The broccoli takes only minutes to cook in a microwave oven. It's topped with toasted almonds.

Tuscan Chicken with Tomato-Basil Relish

1/2 cup diced plum tomatoes
2 tablespoons diced red onion
1/4 cup sliced, drained sweet pimientos
1/4 cup snipped fresh basil leaves
1/2 tablespoon balsamic vinegar
Salt and freshly ground black pepper
3/4 pound boneless, skinless chicken breasts
Olive oil spray

Mix tomatoes, onion, sweet pimientos, and basil together in a small bowl. Add vinegar and toss to mix. Add salt and pepper to taste. Set aside.

Place chicken between two pieces of waxed paper or aluminum foil and flatten with a meat bat or the bottom of a heavy skillet to 1/2 inch thick. Heat a large nonstick skillet on medium-high heat and spray with olive oil spray. Add chicken and sauté 3 minutes per side. Sprinkle salt and pepper to taste on the cooked sides. Divide between 2 dinner plates and spoon the tomato relish on top. Makes 2 servings.

Per serving: 307 calories, 54.6 grams protein, 4.2 grams carbohydrate, 9.0 grams fat (2.1 saturated), 144 milligrams cholesterol, 131 milligrams sodium, 0 gram fiber

Toasted Almond Broccoli

4 tablespoons sliced almonds
1/2 pound broccoli florets (4 cups)
2 teaspoons olive oil
Salt and freshly ground black pepper

Heat a nonstick skillet on medium heat and add almonds. (This can be done in the same skillet to be used for the chicken.) Sauté 1 minute or until almonds are golden, not brown. Remove and set aside. Place broccoli in a microwave-safe bowl and microwave on high for 4 minutes. Remove and add oil and salt and pepper to taste. Toss well. Sprinkle almonds on top.
Makes 2 servings.

Per serving: 213 calories, 9.7 grams protein, 13.4 grams carbohydrate, 16.2 grams fat (1.4 saturated), 0 milligram cholesterol, 40 milligrams sodium, 4.9 grams fiber

stage II
which carbs

When I teach classes, I find that this is the most important section. My students are afraid to start reintroducing carbs for fear they will negate all of the benefits they've achieved. Here's how you can prevent regaining lost weight.

The question that keeps coming up at every class is, "How do I start to add carbohydrates to my meals?" Two things usually happen at this point. You are losing weight and feeling good, so you stay on the Quick Start phase until you get bored or have a special event. Or you think, "Great. I've lost weight and now I can have the foods I love and forget about the carb restrictions." But neither solution leads to a healthy lifestyle of low-carb eating.

This section shows you how to start bringing carbs back into your life without gaining weight. I have carefully chosen these recipes to reincorporate high-fiber, low-simple-sugar carbohydrates. The most important addition in this section is high-fiber cereal in the morning.

As with the other sections, I have organized the menus into a meal-at-a-glance chart incorporating some easy and quick meals from the Super Speed Supper section to accommodate busy midweek schedules and some more elaborate recipes from the Weekend Meals section suited to a more relaxed weekend pace. They are arranged to give variety throughout the day and over the days of the week.

Breakfast

You can choose from a variety of breakfasts to fit your taste. Quick ideas like microwave Ham-Baked Egg with Oatmeal can be done in about 5 minutes. You can also enjoy an Italian Omelet with Bran Cereal.

Lunch

Cajun Shrimp Salad and Oranges and a quick Horseradish-Crusted Grilled Salmon Salad and Apple are two of the tempting choices.

Dinner

Five-Spice Tuna Tataki with Japanese Brown Rice and Raspberry Banana Cooler, and Veal Piccata with Garlic Zucchini and Tomato Orzo, are two of the meals that have been carefully planned to slowly reintroduce carbohydrates.

For those days when you are really pressed for time, select Peasant Country Soup with Herb Cheese Toast and Salad or Swordfish in Spanish Sofrito Sauce with Yellow Rice from the Super Speed Suppers section of the book.

For weekends when you have more time and want something special, try the Steak in Port Wine with French Green Beans and Brown Rice or Chicken and Walnuts in Lettuce Puffs with Sweet and Sour Cabbage and Oranges from the Weekend Meals section of the book.

During the Which Carb 14-Day Meal Plan, which includes the Super Speed Suppers and Weekend Meals, you will consume an average of 85 to 95 grams of carbohydrates per day. Carbohydrate percentage is based on carbohydrates less fiber consumed, which is the normal way of calculating carbohydrate consumption. The balance of these meals is 26 percent of calories from carbohydrates, 35 percent of calories from low-fat protein, 24 percent of calories from monounsaturated fat, and 10 percent of calories from saturated fat.

Which Carbs 14-Day Menu Plan at a Glance

tuscan chicken **p60**

p67 frittata with bran cereal

week 2	breakfast	lunch	dinner
sunday	Tomato, Cheese, and Parsley Frittata with Bran Cereal 67	Italian Croque Monsieur and Watermelon Cubes . . . 75	Chicken and Walnuts in Lettuce Puffs with Sweet and Sour Cabbage and Oranges 157
monday	Roast Beef Cucumber Slices with Bran Cereal 68	Vietnamese Crab Soup and Honeydew Melon 76	Peasant Country Soup with Herb Cheese Toast and Salad 136
tuesday	Sausage Scramble with Oatmeal 69	Cajun Shrimp Salad and Orange 77	Beef Teriyaki with Chinese Noodles 137
wednesday	Ginger-Cranberry Smoothie, Smoked Ham and Cheese, and Bran Cereal 70	Roast Chicken Vegetable Soup and Pineapple .. 78	Five-Spice Tuna Tataki with Japanese Brown Rice and Raspberry Banana Cooler 90
thursday	Ham-Baked Egg with Oatmeal 71	Rainbow Tomato Plate and Yogurt 79	Chicken with Black Bean and Corn Salsa Salad .. 92
friday	Italian Omelet with Bran Cereal 72	Horseradish-Crusted Grilled Salmon Salad and Apple 80	Veal Piccata with Garlic Zucchini and Tomato Orzo 93
saturday	New Orleans Shrimp Roll with Oatmeal 73	Chinese Chicken Salad 81	Steak in Port Wine with French Green Beans and Brown Rice 159

which carbs

breakfasts

Tomato, Cheese, and Parsley Frittata with Bran Cereal

Frittatas take about 10 minutes to make. They can be made ahead and eaten at room temperature. ● *A frittata needs to be cooked on both sides. Some people flip it in the pan. A much easier way is to place it in the oven to finish cooking, under a broiler for half a minute, or use this recipe's method of covering the frittata with a lid.*

Tomato, Cheese, and Parsley Frittata

2 whole eggs

6 egg whites

1 medium tomato, cut into 1-inch pieces

1 teaspoon dried thyme

1 cup fresh parsley, torn into bite-size pieces

Salt and freshly ground black pepper

Olive oil spray

6 tablespoons shredded part-skim milk mozzarella cheese

Lightly beat whole egg and egg whites together. Add tomato, thyme, parsley, and salt and pepper to taste. Heat an 8- to 9-inch nonstick skillet over medium heat and spray with olive oil spray. Pour egg mixture into skillet. Tilt pan until mixture covers skillet. Leave to set on the bottom for 1 minute. Sprinkle cheese on top. Turn heat to low, cover with a lid, and let cook 10 minutes or until set. Cut in half and serve on 2 plates. Makes 2 servings.

Bran Cereal

1 cup skim milk

1 cup high-fiber, no-sugar-added bran cereal

Divide between 2 cereal bowls. Makes 2 servings.

Per serving: 324 calories, 32.8 grams protein, 36.3 grams carbohydrate, 12.9 grams fat (4.9 saturated), 231 milligrams cholesterol, 575 milligrams sodium, 13.0 grams fiber

Helpful Hint

● *Dried thyme is used in this recipe. Replace dried herbs after 6 months. If they look gray and old, that's probably how they will taste.*

Countdown

● *Start frittata.*
● *While frittata cooks, assemble cereal.*
● *Finish frittata.*

Shopping List

Produce

1 medium tomato

1 small bunch parsley

Dairy

1 small package part-skim milk mozzarella cheese

Staples

Dried thyme

Eggs (8 needed)

Skim milk

Olive oil spray

High-fiber, no-sugar-added bran cereal

Salt

Black peppercorns

Helpful Hint

- *Try to cut the cucumber slices on the diagonal. Hold the knife at an angle to the cucumber rather than perpendicular to it. This will give more surface area to sit the roast beef on.*

Countdown

- *Assemble the roast beef slices.*
- *Assemble cereal.*

Shopping List

Produce

1 medium cucumber

Deli

½ pound sliced, lean roast beef

Staples

Skim milk

High-fiber, no-sugar-added bran cereal

Reduced-fat mayonnaise

Salt

Black peppercorns

Roast Beef Cucumber Slices with Bran Cereal

This is a perfect breakfast to eat on the run. The roast beef slices can be made the night before and refrigerated.

Roast Beef Cucumber Slices

1 medium cucumber

2 tablespoons reduced-fat mayonnaise

Salt and freshly ground black pepper

½ pound sliced, lean roast beef

Peel cucumber and slice about ¼ inch thick on the diagonal. Spread mayonnaise on each slice. Sprinkle with salt and pepper to taste. Fold the sliced roast beef to fit the cucumber slices and place on top. Divide between 2 plates. Makes 2 servings.

Bran Cereal

1 cup skim milk

1 cup high-fiber, no-sugar-added bran cereal

Divide between 2 cereal bowls. Makes 2 servings.

Per serving: 391 calories, 39.9 grams protein, 35.5 grams carbohydrate, 15.2 grams fat (4.4 saturated), 100 milligrams cholesterol, 390 milligrams sodium, 13.9 grams fiber

Sausage Scramble with Oatmeal

Lean, mild turkey sausage makes these scrambled eggs special. The sausages come mild or hot. Choose whichever you like.

Sausage Scramble

6 ounces mild or hot, low-fat Italian turkey sausage, cut into ½ inch slices

2 whole eggs

4 egg whites

½ teaspoon dried oregano

Salt and freshly ground black pepper

Heat a medium-size nonstick skillet on medium-high heat. Add sausage slices and cook 3 minutes. While sausage cooks, mix whole eggs and whites together and add oregano and salt and pepper to taste. Add egg mixture to the skillet. Scramble for 1 minute, or until egg is cooked to desired doneness. Makes 2 servings.

Oatmeal

1 cup oatmeal

2 cups water

1 cup skim milk

1 teaspoon cinnamon

Sugar substitute equivalent to 2 teaspoons sugar

To prepare in the microwave, combine oatmeal and water together. Microwave on high for 4 minutes. Stir in milk, cinnamon, and sugar substitute. Makes 2 servings.

Alternatively, combine oatmeal and water in a small saucepan. Bring to a boil. Cook about 5 minutes over medium heat, stirring occasionally. Stir in milk, cinnamon, and sugar substitute. Makes 2 servings.

Per serving: 442 calories, 37.3 grams protein, 37.6 grams carbohydrate, 16.9 grams fat (4.3 saturated), 260 milligrams cholesterol, 777 milligrams sodium, 4.2 grams fiber

Helpful Hint

● *Dried oregano is used in this recipe. Replace dried herbs after 6 months. If they look gray and old, that's probably how they will taste.*

Countdown

● *Make oatmeal.*

● *Make sausage scramble.*

Shopping List

Meat

6 ounces low-fat Italian turkey sausage

Staples

Dried oregano

Eggs (6 needed)

Oatmeal

Skim milk

Cinnamon

Sugar substitute

Salt

Black peppercorns

Ginger-Cranberry Smoothie, Smoked Ham and Cheese, and Bran Cereal

Helpful Hints

- *Frozen or fresh cranberries can be used.*
- *Add a little more water if smoothie is too thick.*
- *Ground ginger is used in this recipe. Replace dried spices after 6 months. They lose their flavor after that time.*

Countdown

- *Make smoothie.*
- *Make oatmeal.*
- *Assemble ham and cheese.*

Shopping List

Produce

1 small bag cranberries or 1 bag frozen cranberries
1 small head lettuce

Dairy

1 package reduced-fat Cheddar cheese
1 small carton nonfat vanilla yogurt

Deli

1 small package smoked, lean ham

Grocery

1 small jar ground ginger

Staples

Skim milk
High-fiber, no-sugar-added bran cereal
Sugar substitute

Ginger gives this colorful smoothie a taste of Asia.

Ginger-Cranberry Smoothie

½ cup fresh or frozen cranberries
¼ cup water
½ cup nonfat vanilla yogurt
1 teaspoon ground ginger
Sugar substitute equivalent to 4 teaspoons sugar
2 cups ice cubes

Place cranberries, water, yogurt, ginger, and sugar substitute in a blender. Blend until smooth. Add the ice cubes and blend until thick. Pour into 2 glasses. Makes 2 servings.

Smoked Ham and Cheese

Several lettuce leaves
½ pound smoked, lean ham, cut into ½-inch cubes
2 ounces reduced-fat Cheddar cheese, torn into bite-size pieces

Place lettuce on 2 plates with ham and cheese sprinkled on top. Makes 2 servings.

Bran Cereal

1 cup skim milk
1 cup high-fiber, no-sugar-added bran cereal

Divide between 2 cereal bowls. Makes 2 servings.

Per serving: 394 calories, 38.4 grams protein, 42.6 grams carbohydrate, 13.1 grams fat (6.2 saturated), 76 milligrams cholesterol, 1473 milligrams sodium, 14.2 grams fiber

Ham-Baked Egg with Oatmeal

Baked or shirred eggs are easy to make and are a nice change. They take about 12 to 15 minutes in the oven. I've shortened the time to 2 minutes by "baking" them in a microwave oven. The secret is to gently prick the egg yolk in 2 places to break the membrane before placing in the microwave oven.

Ham-Baked Egg

2 teaspoons olive oil
½ pound lean ham torn into
    bite-size pieces
2 whole eggs
Salt and freshly ground black
    pepper

Spoon oil into 2 small ramekins. Divide ham into 2 portions and place in the ramekins. Break 1 egg into each dish. With the tip of a very sharp knife make 2 tiny pricks in each egg yolk, just to break the membrane and let steam escape. Sprinkle with salt and pepper to taste. Place one ramekin in a microwave oven. Cover ramekin with a paper towel and microwave on high for 1 minute. Remove and serve. Repeat with second ramekin. Makes 2 servings.

Oatmeal

1 cup oatmeal
2 cups water
1 cup skim milk
Sugar substitute equivalent
    to 2 teaspoons sugar

To prepare in the microwave, combine oatmeal and water together. Microwave on high for 4 minutes. Stir in milk and sugar substitute. Makes 2 serving.

Alternatively, combine oatmeal and water in a small saucepan. Bring to a boil. Lower heat to medium and cook about 5 minutes, stirring occasionally. Stir in milk and sugar substitute. Makes 2 servings.

Per serving: 458 calories, 37.2 grams protein, 35.7 grams carbohydrate, 19.1 grams fat (4.9 saturated), 268 milligrams cholesterol, 1110 milligrams sodium, 4 grams fiber

Helpful Hints

- *Cook the eggs for 1½ minutes each (3 minutes total) for a firmer yolk.*
- *Small dessert or glass bowls can be used instead of ramekins. They should measure about 3- to 4-inches wide and 2-inches deep.*

Countdown

- *Assemble eggs and ham in ramekins.*
- *Assemble cereal.*
- *Microwave eggs.*

Shopping List

Deli
    ½ pound lean, smoked ham

Staples
    Eggs (2 needed)
    Skim milk
    Olive oil
    Oatmeal
    Salt
    Black peppercorns
    Sugar substitute

Italian Omelet with Bran Cereal

Helpful Hint

- Buy good-quality Parmesan cheese and ask the market to grate it for you or chop it in your food processor. Freeze extra for quick use. You can quickly spoon out what you need and leave the rest frozen.

Countdown

- Prepare omelet ingredients.
- Assemble bran cereal.
- Make omelet.

Shopping List

Dairy

1 small carton nonfat ricotta cheese

Grocery

1 small bottle low-sugar, low-fat chunky marinara sauce

Staples

Egg substitute

Parmesan cheese

Skim milk

Olive oil

High-fiber, no-sugar-added bran cereal

Black peppercorns

A perfect omelet is golden on the top with a delicate creamy center. The secret is to cook it over medium-high heat for only a couple of minutes while gently scraping the side to make sure all of the egg is cooked.

Italian Omelet

¼ cup nonfat ricotta cheese
¼ cup bottled low-sugar, low-fat chunky marinara sauce
¼ cup grated Parmesan cheese
1½ cups egg substitute
Freshly ground black pepper
2 teaspoons olive oil

Mix ricotta cheese, marinara sauce, and Parmesan cheese together and set aside. Mix egg substitute with pepper to taste. Heat oil in a medium-size nonstick skillet on medium-high heat. Pour in the egg mixture. Let the eggs set for about 30 seconds. Tip the pan and lightly move the eggs until they all set. Spread the cheese mixture on half the omelet and fold the omelet in half. Slide out of the pan by tipping the pan and holding a plate vertically against the side of the pan. Turn the pan and plate to invert the omelet onto the plate. Cut in half and serve on 2 plates. Makes 2 servings.

Bran Cereal

1 cup skim milk
1 cup high-fiber, no-sugar-added bran cereal

Divide between 2 cereal bowls. Makes 2 servings.

Per serving: 365 calories, 32.6 grams protein, 36.8 grams carbohydrate, 12.4 grams fat (4.5 saturated), 17 milligrams cholesterol, 1076 milligrams sodium, 13.0 grams fiber

New Orleans Shrimp Roll with Oatmeal

Shrimp and hot pepper sauce give this rollup a hint of New Orleans cooking. The egg is cooked like a crepe and used as a wrap.

New Orleans Shrimp Roll

½ pound cooked shrimp, peeled and deveined
2 tablespoons mayonnaise
Several drops hot pepper sauce
Salt and freshly ground black pepper
1 cup egg substitute
Olive oil spray

Coarsely chop shrimp. Add mayonnaise and hot pepper sauce. Add salt and pepper to taste. Mix egg substitute with salt and pepper to taste. Heat a medium-size nonstick skillet on medium-high heat. Spray with olive oil spray and pour ½ cup egg substitute into the skillet and spread to make a thin layer. Let cook 2 minutes. Turn over for 1 minute. Remove from heat. Spread half of shrimp mixture on top. Roll up and place on a plate. Repeat for second serving. Makes 2 servings.

Oatmeal

1 cup oatmeal
2 cups water
1 cup skim milk
Sugar substitute equivalent to 2 teaspoons sugar

To prepare in the microwave, combine oatmeal and water together. Microwave on high for 4 minutes. Stir in milk and sugar substitute. Makes 2 servings.

Alternatively, combine oatmeal and water in a small saucepan. Bring to a boil. Cook about 5 minutes over medium heat, stirring occasionally. Stir in milk and sugar substitute. Makes 2 servings.

Per serving: 473 calories, 44.3 grams protein, 36.5 grams carbohydrate, 16.0 grams fat (2.6 saturated), 180 milligrams cholesterol, 535 milligrams sodium, 4 grams fiber

Helpful Hints

- *Cooked, shelled shrimp can be found in the fish department or frozen in most supermarkets.*
- *Use the pulse button on a food processor to coarsely chop the shrimp.*

Countdown

- *Prepare shrimp filling.*
- *Make shrimp roll.*
- *Assemble cereal.*

Shopping List

Seafood
 ¾ pound cooked, peeled, deveined shrimp

Staples
 Mayonnaise
 Egg substitute
 Olive oil spray
 Hot pepper sauce
 Skim milk
 Oatmeal
 Sugar substitute
 Salt
 Black peppercorns

which carbs
lunches

Grilled Ham and Cheese Italiano and Watermelon Cubes

Nearly every brasserie in Paris serves a version of grilled ham and cheese sandwich (croque monsieur). Here is an Italian version.

Italian Croque Monsieur

Olive oil spray
4 slices whole wheat bread
¼ pound part-skim milk mozzarella cheese, sliced
½ pound lean ham, sliced
1 medium tomato, sliced, patted dry on paper towel
½ cup fresh basil, torn into bite-size pieces (optional)

Preheat broiler. Line a baking sheet with aluminum foil and spray with olive oil spray. Place bread on foil and spray bread. Place cheese and then ham on bread. Top with sliced tomato. Broil 2 minutes or until cheese melts. Remove and sprinkle with basil. Makes 2 servings.

Per serving: 424 calories, 44.7 grams protein, 26.3 grams carbohydrate, 18.9 grams fat (8.3 saturated), 86 milligrams cholesterol, 1483 milligrams sodium, 6.0 grams fiber

Watermelon Cubes

2 cups watermelon cubes

Divide between 2 small dessert dishes. Makes 2 servings.

Per serving: 49 calories, 1.0 gram protein, 11.0 grams carbohydrate, 0.6 gram fat (0.1 saturated), 0 milligram cholesterol, 3 milligrams sodium, 0.8 gram fiber

Helpful Hint

- *Watermelon cubes can be found in the produce section or on the salad bar of most supermarkets.*

Countdown

- *Preheat broiler.*
- *Make sandwich.*
- *While sandwich toasts, place watermelon in dishes.*

Shopping List

Produce
1 small bunch basil
1 medium tomato
1 small container watermelon cubes

Dairy
1 small package part-skim milk mozzarella cheese

Deli
½ pound lean ham

Staples
Olive oil spray
Whole wheat bread

Vietnamese Crab Soup and Honeydew Melon Cubes

Helpful Hints

- If fresh crab is unavailable, use good-quality pasteurized crab or shrimp.
- One tablespoon lime juice can be substituted for the lemongrass.
- A quick way to chop ginger is to peel, cut into chunks, and press through a garlic press with large holes. Press over food or bowl to catch juices as ginger is pressed. The ginger pulp will not go through a small garlic press. Just the juice is enough to flavor the dish.
- Cubed fresh honeydew can be found in the produce section of most supermarkets.

Countdown

- Assemble ingredients for soup.
- Place melon cubes in dessert dishes.
- Complete soup.

Shopping List

Produce
1 small bunch lemongrass (2 stalks needed)
1 lime
5 ounces fresh snow peas
1 small bag bean sprouts
1 small bunch scallions
1 small container fresh honeydew cubes
1 small piece fresh ginger

Seafood
¾ pound fresh or pasteurized crabmeat

Grocery
1 small bottle sesame oil

Staples
Fat-free, low-sodium chicken broth
Hot pepper sauce
Salt
Black peppercorns

This soup is filled with the fragrant flavors of Southeast Asia. As with most Asian dishes, it takes a little longer to prepare the ingredients, but then it takes less than 5 minutes to cook.
- Lemongrass, which adds a special lemon flavor to Asian dishes, can be found in some supermarkets. It looks something like a scallion, but the stalks are a pale green color, hard, and dry. Use the white bulbous end for the soup.

Vietnamese Crab Soup

2 cups fat-free, low-sodium chicken broth
2 cups water
2 stalks lemongrass, tender white base only, sliced
1 tablespoon peeled and coarsely chopped fresh ginger
1 tablespoon lime zest (grated skin)
5 ounces fresh snow peas, trimmed (2 cups)
1 cup bean sprouts
¾ pound fresh or pasteurized crabmeat, drained
2 tablespoons sesame oil
Several drops hot pepper sauce
Salt and freshly ground black pepper
2 scallions, sliced (½ cup)

Place chicken broth and water in a large saucepan. Add lemongrass, ginger, lime zest, and snow peas. Bring to a simmer on medium heat and cook 2 minutes. Add bean sprouts and crab. Simmer 2 more minutes. Remove from heat and add sesame oil, hot pepper sauce, and salt and pepper to taste. Ladle into 2 soup bowls and sprinkle scallions on top. Makes 2 servings.

Per serving: 343 calories, 37.3 grams protein, 11.8 grams carbohydrate, 15.8 grams fat (2.2 saturated), 133 milligrams cholesterol, 1070 milligrams sodium, 2.6 grams fiber

Honeydew Melon Cubes

2 cups honeydew cubes

Divide between 2 small dessert plates. Makes 2 servings.

Per serving: 57 calories, 1.4 grams protein, 13.4 grams carbohydrate, 0.4 gram fat (0 saturated), 0 milligram cholesterol, 14 milligrams sodium, 0.5 gram fiber

Cajun Shrimp Salad and Orange Segments

The hot spices of Louisiana Cajun country flavor this quick shrimp salad.

Cajun Shrimp Salad

2 tablespoons no-sugar-added oil
   (olive or canola) and vinegar
   dressing
2 garlic cloves, crushed
½ teaspoon cayenne
1 teaspoon dried oregano
1 teaspoon dried thyme
¾ pound cooked shrimp, peeled,
   deveined, and cut in half
   (about 2 cups)
1 small head romaine lettuce heart
1 medium red pepper, cut into
   small cubes (1 cup)

In a small bowl, mix dressing with garlic, cayenne, oregano, and thyme. Add shrimp and toss well. Tear lettuce into bite-size pieces and place on 2 plates. Mix red pepper with shrimp and spoon shrimp and dressing over lettuce. Makes 2 servings.

Per serving: 301 calories, 37.2 grams protein, 10.6 grams carbohydrate, 11.7 grams fat (1.9 saturated), 260 milligrams cholesterol, 342 milligrams sodium, 0.9 grams fiber

Orange Segments

2 oranges

Peel and separate into segments. Divide between 2 small plates. Makes 2 servings.

Per serving: 62 calories, 1.2 grams protein, 15.4 grams carbohydrate, 0.2 gram fat (0 saturated), 0 milligram cholesterol, 0 milligram sodium, 3.1 grams fiber

Helpful Hints

- Cooked, shelled shrimp can be found in the fish department or frozen in the frozen section of most supermarkets.
- Prepared Cajun spice mix can be used instead of the spice mixture in the recipe. Make sure no sugar or salt is added to the mixture.
- Dried oregano, thyme and cayenne pepper are used in this recipe. Replace dried herbs after 6 months. If they look gray and old, that's probably how they will taste.

Countdown

- Make dressing.
- Complete salad.

Shopping List

Produce
1 small head romaine lettuce heart
1 medium red pepper
2 oranges

Seafood
¾ pound cooked, peeled, and deveined shrimp

Staples
Dried thyme
Dried oregano
Cayenne pepper
No-sugar-added oil (olive or canola) and vinegar dressing
Garlic

Roast Chicken Vegetable Soup and Pineapple Cubes

A cheery bowl of soup is a treat any time of year. This soup uses roasted, ready-to-eat chicken and can be ready in less than 15 minutes. The soup tastes great the second day. Make extra if you have time and save for a second day or freeze.

Roast Chicken Vegetable Soup

2 teaspoons olive oil
½ cup sliced yellow onion
1 celery stalk, sliced (½ cup)
½ pound mushrooms, sliced (3 cups)
2 cups fat-free, low-sodium chicken broth
1 cup water
2 large sprigs fresh thyme or 1 teaspoon dried thyme
½ pound roasted, ready-to-eat chicken pieces (about 1¾ cups)
Salt and freshly ground black pepper
2 tablespoons grated Parmesan cheese

Heat oil in a large saucepan over medium high heat and add onion and celery. Sauté 3 minutes. Add mushrooms, broth, water, and thyme. Reduce heat to medium and simmer 7 minutes. Add chicken and cook 2 minutes or until chicken is warmed through. Remove thyme sprigs and add salt and pepper to taste. Spoon into 2 soup bowls and sprinkle Parmesan cheese on top. Makes 2 servings.

Per serving: 334 calories, 44.8 grams protein, 8.3 grams carbohydrate, 13.5 grams fat (3.6 saturated), 103 milligrams cholesterol, 858 milligrams sodium, 0.5 gram fiber

Pineapple Cubes

2 cups pineapple cubes

Divide between 2 dessert dishes. Makes 2 servings.

Per serving: 77 calories, 0.6 gram protein, 19.2 grams carbohydrate, 0.7 gram fat (0 saturated), 0 milligram cholesterol, 1 milligram sodium, 2.4 grams fiber

Rainbow Tomato Plate and Fruit Yogurt

This colorful salad plate accented with red and yellow tomatoes takes only 5 minutes to assemble.

Rainbow Tomato Plate

2 small red tomatoes, sliced

2 small yellow tomatoes, sliced

1 medium cucumber, peeled and sliced

¼ cup pine nuts

6 ounces smoked chicken breast, cut into cubes (about 1½ cups)

2 tablespoons no-sugar-added oil (olive or canola) and vinegar dressing

Salt and freshly ground black pepper

Arrange the sliced tomatoes and cucumber in circles on 2 plates, alternating red tomato slices, yellow tomato slices, and cucumber slices. The slices should cover the plate. Sprinkle chicken cubes and pine nuts over tomatoes. Drizzle dressing over the top. Sprinkle with salt and pepper to taste. Makes 2 servings.

> Per serving: 354 calories, 32.1 grams protein, 15.1 grams carbohydrate, 13.0 grams fat (2.2 saturated), 72 milligrams cholesterol, 161 milligrams sodium, 0.9 gram fiber

Fruit Yogurt

1 cup light fruit yogurt

Divide yogurt between 2 small dessert bowls. Makes 2 servings.

> Per serving: 70 calories, 5.5 grams protein, 11.5 grams carbohydrate, 0 gram fat (0 saturated), 3 milligrams cholesterol, 95 milligrams sodium, 0 gram fiber

Helpful Hints

- *Any type of tomatoes can be used.*
- *Any flavor nonfat yogurt can be used for dessert.*
- *Extra pine nuts can be stored in the freezer.*

Countdown

- *Make salad plate.*
- *Serve yogurt.*

Shopping List

Produce

2 small red tomatoes

2 small yellow tomatoes

1 medium cucumber

Dairy

1 (8-ounce) carton light fruit yogurt

Deli

6 ounces smoked chicken breast

Grocery

1 small package pine nuts

Staples

No-sugar-added oil (olive or canola) and vinegar dressing

Salt

Black peppercorns

Horseradish-Crusted Grilled Salmon Salad and Apple Slices

A spicy, creamy crust covers the rich salmon fillet for this quick lunch. The salmon tastes great hot or served at room temperature.

Horseradish-Crusted Salmon Salad

Olive oil spray
½ pound salmon fillet
Salt and freshly ground black pepper
2 tablespoons prepared horseradish
2 tablespoons mayonnaise
4 cups washed, ready-to-eat romaine leaves
1 medium cucumber, peeled and sliced

Preheat broiler. Line a baking sheet with aluminum foil and spray with olive oil spray. Place salmon on the sheet. Sprinkle with salt and pepper to taste. Broil 3 minutes. Mix horseradish and mayonnaise together. Remove salmon and turn over. Spread with horseradish mixture. Return to boiler for 3 minutes. Place lettuce and cucumber on 2 plates. Remove salmon and divide in half. Place over greens. Makes 2 servings.

Per serving: 340 calories, 30.4 grams protein, 8.7 grams carbohydrate, 19.3 grams fat (3.4 saturated), 85 milligrams cholesterol, 181 milligrams sodium, 1.5 grams fiber

Apple Slices

2 medium apples

Core and slice apples. Serve 1 apple per person. Makes 2 servings.

Per serving: 81 calories, 0.3 gram protein, 21.1 grams carbohydrate, 0.5 gram fat (0.1 saturated), 0 milligram cholesterol, 0 milligram sodium, 3.7 grams fiber rainbow tomato plate   p79

Chinese Chicken Salad

Adding five-spice powder and soy sauce to a bottled oil and vinegar dressing gives this salad an aromatic Chinese flavor.

1 tablespoon low-sodium
  soy sauce

½ teaspoon five-spice powder

2 tablespoons no-sugar-added
  oil (olive or canola) and vinegar
  dressing

1 cup bean sprouts

½ pound roasted, ready-to-eat
  chicken pieces

Salt and freshly ground
  black pepper

3 cups sliced Chinese cabbage

4 tangerines, peeled and
  segmented

In a medium-size bowl, mix soy sauce, five-spice powder, and dressing together. Add the bean sprouts and chicken and toss well. Add salt and pepper to taste. Place cabbage on 2 plates and spoon chicken mixture on top. Sprinkle tangerine segments on top. Makes 2 servings.

Per serving: 388 calories, 40.6 grams protein, 28.9 grams carbohydrate, 14.5 grams fat (2.5 saturated), 96 milligrams cholesterol, 485 milligrams sodium, 2.4 grams fiber

Helpful Hints

- Chinese cabbage is also called napa cabbage.
- Any type of lettuce can be used.

Countdown

- Mix dressing ingredients together.
- Complete salad.
- Assemble dessert.

Shopping List

Produce

1 small Chinese cabbage (napa cabbage)

1 small container fresh bean sprouts

4 tangerines

Meat or Deli

½ pound roasted, ready-to-eat chicken pieces

Grocery

1 small jar five-spice powder

Staples

Low-sodium soy sauce

No-sugar-added oil (olive or canola) and vinegar dressing

Salt

Black peppercorns

which carbs

dinners

Crispy Mahi Mahi with Ratatouille and Pumpkin Pudding

For this quick meal, freshly made ratatouille—a tasty blend of Provençal vegetables—is combined with juicy fish fillets. Coating the fish fillet with coarse cornmeal gives it a crispy crust without deep-frying it. ● I am often asked how to cook fish so that it's juicy and not dried out. The general rule is to cook fish 10 minutes for each inch of thickness. If the fish is thicker than 1 inch, cook it a little longer, or if thinner, cook it a shorter time.

Crispy Mahi Mahi

¾ pound Mahi Mahi fillet
2 tablespoons coarse cornmeal
Salt and freshly ground black
    pepper
2 teaspoons olive oil

Wash fillet and pat dry with paper towel. Season cornmeal with salt and pepper to taste. Dip fillet into cornmeal, making sure both sides are well coated. Heat olive oil in a medium-size nonstick skillet on medium-high heat. Add mahi mahi and sauté 5 minutes. Turn and sauté 5 minutes for a 1-inch thick fillet. Reduce cooking time to 8 total minutes for ½-inch fillet. Divide in half and serve. Makes 2 servings.

> Per serving: 203 calories, 29.3 grams protein, 5.6 grams carbohydrate, 6.0 grams fat (1.0 saturated), 116 milligrams cholesterol, 136 milligrams sodium, 0 gram fiber

Ratatouille (Sautéed Provençal Vegetables)

6 ounces eggplant, washed,
    unpeeled, and sliced
    (1¾ to 2 cups)
6 ounces zucchini, washed and
    sliced (1½ cups)
½ cup sliced red onion
2 medium garlic cloves, crushed
2 cups low sodium, no-sugar-
    added tomato or pasta sauce
½ cup water
2 teaspoons olive oil
Salt and freshly ground
    black pepper

Add eggplant, zucchini, onion, garlic, tomato sauce, and water to a medium-size saucepan. Bring to a simmer over medium-high heat. Lower heat and cover. Simmer 15 minutes. Vegetables should be cooked through but a little firm. Stir in olive oil and add salt and pepper to taste. Makes 2 servings.

> Per serving: 223 calories, 5.9 grams protein, 18.9 grams carbohydrate, 4.7 grams fat (0.6 saturated), 0 milligram cholesterol, 44 milligrams sodium, 3.5 grams fiber

continues

Helpful Hints

- Cornmeal can be found in three textures—coarse, medium, or fine; and three colors—white, yellow, or blue, depending on the type of corn used. White and yellow cornmeal can be found in most supermarkets. Any type can be used.
- You can use cod, haddock, bass, or grouper in place of the mahi mahi called for.
- For the pumpkin pudding, use the mixture of spices given or use premixed pumpkin pie spice mixture, making sure no sugar has been added.

Countdown

- Start ratatouille.
- Make pumpkin pudding.
- Prepare mahi mahi.

Crispy Mahi Mahi with Ratatouille and Pumpkin Pudding continued

continued

Shopping List

Produce
6 ounces eggplant
6 ounces zucchini

Dairy
1 (8-ounce) carton nonfat vanilla yogurt

Seafood
¾ pound mahi mahi fillets

Grocery
1 small package coarse cornmeal
1 small can 100% pure pumpkin
1 small package pecan pieces

Staples
Red onion
Garlic
Olive oil
Low-sodium, no-sugar-added tomato or pasta sauce
Sugar substitute
Ground cinnamon
Ground nutmeg
Salt
Black peppercorns

Pumpkin Pudding

¾ cup canned 100% pure pumpkin
¾ cup nonfat vanilla yogurt
⅛ teaspoon ground cinnamon
⅛ teaspoon ground nutmeg
Sugar substitute equivalent to 2 teaspoons sugar
2 tablespoons pecan pieces, toasted

Mix together pumpkin, cinnamon, nutmeg, and sugar substitute. Fold into yogurt. Toast pecan pieces in a toaster oven or under a broiler until golden, about 2 minutes. Divide pumpkin mixture between 2 small dessert bowls or ramekins and sprinkle pecans on top. Makes 2 servings.

Per serving: 162 calories, 6.2 grams protein, 18.4 grams carbohydrate, 8.4 grams fat (0.9 saturated), 2 milligrams cholesterol, 73 milligrams sodium, 3.7 grams fiber

Eggplant Parmesan over Linguine

Eggplant Parmesan, my husband's favorite dish, is a Neapolitan dish made with slices of eggplant baked in a rich tomato sauce and Parmesan cheese. Normally, this dish requires the time-consuming step of frying the eggplant before it's baked. I've created this quick version by microwaving the slices instead. I also found that it makes the dish much lighter than fried or sautéed eggplant, which tends to soak up a lot of oil during the cooking.

½ pound eggplant, cut into
　　¼-inch slices (about 3 cups)

Olive oil spray

Salt and freshly ground
　　black pepper

1½ cups low-sodium, no-sugar-
　　added, tomato sauce

6 ounces lean ground round

1 cup arugula leaves

½ cup part-skim milk ricotta
　　cheese

3 tablespoons water

3 tablespoons grated Parmesan
　　cheese

¼ pound whole wheat linguine

2 teaspoons olive oil

Preheat the broiler. Bring a large saucepan filled with 3 to 4 quarts of water to a boil. Arrange eggplant slices on a 9- to 10-inch microwave-safe pie plate. Spray with olive oil spray and sprinkle with salt and pepper to taste. Cover with plastic wrap or a plate. Microwave on high for 3 minutes. Carefully remove cover. Remove sliced eggplant to a plate and set aside.

Mix tomato sauce and ground round together in a microwave-safe bowl. Microwave on high for 3 minutes. Spoon a layer of meat sauce into the bottom of the pie plate. Place arugula leaves over sauce. Place a layer of eggplant slices over the sauce and sprinkle with a little salt and pepper to taste. Repeat with the sauce, eggplant, and salt and pepper. Mix ricotta cheese with water to form a sauce consistency. Add a little more water, if necessary. Spoon ricotta cheese over top of eggplant dish. Sprinkle Parmesan cheese over the ricotta cheese. Broil 5 minutes or until sauce is bubbly and cheese melted.

Place linguine in boiling water for 9 minutes. Drain and toss with olive oil and add salt and pepper to taste.

Place linguine on 2 dinner plates and serve Eggplant Parmesan on top. Makes 2 servings.

Per serving: 597 calories, 53.3 grams protein, 50.1 grams carbohydrate, 19.1 grams fat (10.1 saturated), 122 milligrams cholesterol, 446 milligrams sodium, 9.1 grams fiber

Helpful Hints

- *Buy good-quality Parmesan cheese and ask the market to grate it for you or chop it in your food processor. Freeze extra for quick use. You can quickly spoon out what you need and leave the rest frozen.*
- *This dish can be prepared and assembled in the baking dish in advance and refrigerated several hours or overnight. Bring to room temperature and broil as needed.*

Countdown

- *Preheat broiler.*
- *Boil water for pasta.*
- *Microwave eggplant.*
- *Mix cheese together.*
- *Assemble Eggplant Parmesan dish and place under broiler.*
- *Boil linguine.*

Shopping List

Produce
　½ pound eggplant
　1 small bunch arugula

Dairy
　1 small package part-skim milk ricotta cheese

Meat
　6 ounces lean ground round

Grocery
　1 small package whole wheat linguine (2 ounces needed)

Staples
　Parmesan cheese
　Olive oil spray
　Low-sodium, no-sugar-added tomato or pasta sauce (12 ounces needed)
　Salt
　Black peppercorns

Mediterranean Steak with Minted Couscous and Spiced Peaches

Sautéed steak flavored with the bountiful produce of the Mediterranean provides a quick, 15-minute dinner. ● *Precooked, packaged couscous takes only 5 minutes to make. It's made from semolina flour and is really a form of pasta rather than a grain as many people think. You just boil water, remove from heat, add the couscous, cover, and let stand. For this dinner, I've added fresh mint and chopped tomatoes to add a fresh flavor that goes well with the steak.*

Mediterranean Steak

¾ pound steak (strip, flank, or skirt)
¼ teaspoon cayenne pepper
Olive oil spray
3 tablespoons sliced pimiento-stuffed green olives
2 tablespoons capers
Salt and freshly ground black pepper

Remove fat from steak and sprinkle both sides with cayenne. Heat skillet over medium-high heat. Spray a small, nonstick skillet with olive oil spray. Brown steak 2 minutes per side. Sprinkle olives and capers into skillet and over steak. Lower heat to medium and cook 2 minutes for medium-rare. Cook 2 minutes longer for thick steak. Add salt and pepper to taste.

To serve, place couscous on 2 dinner plates, carve steak, and place on top. Spoon any pan juices over steak. Makes 2 servings.

> Per serving: 356 calories, 55.8 grams protein, 0.3 gram carbohydrate, 16.4 grams fat (7.1 saturated), 140 milligrams cholesterol, 548 milligrams sodium, 0 gram fiber

Minted Couscous

½ cup water
⅓ cup couscous
1 small tomato, diced (1 cup)
3 cups cubed cucumber
¼ cup chopped fresh mint
Salt and freshly ground black pepper

Bring water to a boil. Remove from heat and add couscous, tomatoes, and cucumber. Cover with a lid and let stand 5 minutes. When ready, fluff with a fork. Add mint and salt and pepper to taste. Makes 2 servings.

> Per serving: 144 calories, 5.9 grams protein, 30.0 grams carbohydrate, 0.9 gram fat (0 saturated), 0 milligram cholesterol, 11 milligrams sodium, 1.9 grams fiber

continues

Spiced Peaches

2 medium peaches, pitted
and sliced
½ teaspoon cinnamon
¼ teaspoon allspice
Sugar substitute equivalent
to 1 teaspoon sugar
2 sprigs fresh mint

Arrange peach slices in a circle on 2 small microwavable dessert plates. Mix cinnamon, allspice, and sugar substitute together. Sprinkle mixture over peach slices. Microwave on high for 1 minute. Remove, garnish with mint, and serve. Makes 2 servings.

Per serving: 39 calories, 0.6 gram protein, 10.7 grams carbohydrate, 0.1 gram fat (0 saturated), 0 milligram cholesterol, 0 milligram sodium, 0.5 gram fiber

Shopping List

Produce
1 small bunch fresh mint
1 small tomato
2 medium peaches
1 small cucumber

Meat
¾ pound steak (strip, flank, or skirt)

Grocery
1 small package couscous
1 small jar/can sliced pimiento-stuffed green olives
1 small jar capers
1 small jar allspice

Staples
Olive oil spray
Cayenne pepper
Ground cinnamon
Sugar substitute
Salt
Black peppercorns

Helpful Hints

- *Your wok or skillet should be very hot so the veal will be crisp, not steamed.*
- *Peel and segment grapefruit over a bowl to catch the juice. This will give you the 2 tablespoons of grapefruit juice needed for the recipe.*
- *The grapefruit segments should be about the same size as the veal. If they are too large, cut them in half.*
- *Bought grapefruit segments can be used. Make sure they are natural, without added sugar.*
- *Oyster sauce can be bought in the Asian section of most supermarkets.*

Countdown

- *Marinate veal.*
- *Boil rice.*
- *Prepare all of the stir-fry ingredients.*
- *Stir-fry veal dish.*
- *Finish snow peas and rice.*

Quick-Fried Diced Veal with Snow Peas and Rice

A stir-fry dish with a mystery flavor makes a delicious, quick dinner. The grapefruit nearly melts away leaving an intriguing flavor and texture. ● Stir-fry dishes take a little extra time to prepare the ingredients, but take only a few minutes to cook. I find it is best to line up all of the stir-fry ingredients on a plate or cutting board in order of use. You won't have to keep referring to the recipe while cooking. ● Brown rice takes about 45 minutes to cook. There are several brands of quick-cooking brown rice available. Their cooking times range from 10 minutes to 30 minutes. I find the 30-minute rice has more flavor, but any quick-cooking brown rice will work for this dinner.

Quick-Fried Diced Veal

Sugar substitute equivalent to
   2 teaspoons sugar

2 tablespoons oyster sauce

2 medium garlic cloves, crushed

¾ pound veal cutlets, cut into
   1-inch pieces

1 teaspoon cornstarch

2 teaspoons sesame oil

½ medium cucumber, peeled and
   cut into 1-inch pieces (1½ cups)

1 medium grapefruit, cut into
   segments

2 tablespoons unsweetened
   grapefruit juice from fresh
   grapefruit

Salt and freshly ground
   black pepper

Mix the sugar substitute, oyster sauce, and garlic together. Marinate the veal in the mixture for 10 minutes. Sprinkle cornstarch over veal and toss. Marinade will be absorbed by the veal.

Heat sesame oil in a wok or frying pan. Make sure wok is very hot. Add veal and stir-fry 2 minutes. Remove from wok and add cucumber, grapefruit, and grapefruit juice. Boil to thicken sauce 1 minute. Return veal to wok and remove from heat. Add salt and pepper to taste. Serve over snow peas and rice. Makes 2 servings.

Per serving: 483 calories, 46.4 grams protein, 19.3 grams carbohydrate, 22.9 grams fat (11.6 saturated), 150 milligrams cholesterol, 370 milligrams sodium, 1.8 grams fiber

continues

Snow Peas and Rice

⅓ cup 30-minute quick-cooking
    brown rice
¼ pound snow peas, trimmed
    (2 cups)
1 teaspoon sesame oil
Salt and freshly ground
    black pepper

Fill a large saucepan with about 2 to 3 quarts water. Add rice and bring to a boil. Boil 20 minutes and add snow peas. Continue to boil 2 to 3 minutes. Drain. Toss with sesame oil and salt and pepper to taste. Serve with the veal. Makes 2 servings.

Per serving: 132 calories, 4.3 grams protein, 22.3 grams carbohydrate, 3.2 grams fat (0.5 saturated), 0 milligram cholesterol, 3 milligrams sodium, 2.6 grams fiber

Shopping List

Produce
    ¼ pound snow peas
    1 medium cucumber
    1 medium grapefruit

Meat
    ¾ pound veal cutlets

Grocery
    1 small bottle oyster sauce
    1 small bottle sesame oil

Staples
    30-minute quick-cooking
        brown rice
    Garlic
    Sugar substitute
    Cornstarch
    Salt
    Black peppercorns

Five-Spice Tuna Tataki with Japanese Brown Rice and Raspberry Banana Cooler

Helpful Hints

- *Cracked pepper and five-spice powder can be bought in the spice section of the supermarket.*
- *Red radishes can be used instead of the daikon (white) radish.*

Countdown

- *Sear tuna and let cool slightly.*
- *Make rice.*
- *While rice cooks, prepare sauce.*
- *Make Raspberry Banana Cooler just before serving.*

Tataki, beef or fish that has been seared, thinly sliced, chilled, and served with a dipping sauce, is a tangy, Japanese recipe. Traditional tataki accompaniments are grated daikon (white radish), ginger, chopped scallions, and a dipping sauce. ● *Japanese and Chinese rice vinegar are made from fermented rice. They're milder than most Western vinegars. White vinegar can be substituted in this recipe, but add a few drops of water to soften the flavor.* ● *Brown rice takes about 45 minutes to cook. There are several brands of quick-cooking brown rice available. Their cooking times range from 10 to 30 minutes. I find the 30-minute rice has more flavor, but any quick-cooking rice will work for this dinner.*

Five-Spice Tuna Tataki

2 (6-ounce) tuna steaks
1 tablespoon cracked black pepper
1 1/2 tablespoons sesame oil, divided use
2 tablespoons low-sodium soy sauce
2 medium garlic cloves, crushed
1/4 teaspoon five-spice powder
1/2 cup grated daikon (white) radish (optional)

Roll tuna steaks in cracked black pepper. Heat 1/2 tablespoon sesame oil in a small nonstick skillet over high heat. Sear tuna for 2 minutes. Turn and sear second side 2 minutes. Remove to a cutting board and thinly slice.

Mix soy sauce, remaining tablespoon sesame oil, garlic, and five-spice powder together in a small bowl. Serve sliced tuna on 2 individual dinner plates and spoon sauce on top. Sprinkle with grated daikon radish. Makes 2 servings.

> Per serving: 335 calories, 37.3 grams protein, 2.5 grams carbohydrate, 18.0 grams fat (3.4 saturated), 59 milligrams cholesterol, 677 milligrams sodium, 0 gram fiber

Japanese Brown Rice

1/3 cup 30-minute quick-cooking brown rice
1/4 pound button mushrooms, sliced (1 1/2 cups)
1/4 pound fresh snow peas, trimmed (2 cups)
1/2 cup fat-free, low-sodium chicken broth
1 tablespoon rice vinegar
2 tablespoons low-sodium soy sauce
Salt and freshly ground black pepper

Bring a large saucepan with 2 to 3 quarts of water to a boil. Add rice and boil 25 minutes. Add mushrooms and snow peas and continue to boil 5 minutes. Drain. Mix chicken broth, vinegar, and soy sauce together and toss with rice and vegetables. Add salt and pepper to taste. Makes 2 servings.

> Per serving: 125 calories, 6.1 grams protein, 22.1 grams carbohydrate, 1.1 grams fat (0.1 saturated), 0 milligram cholesterol, 750 milligrams sodium, 2.4 grams fiber

continues

Raspberry Banana Cooler

1 cup frozen raspberries (not in sugar syrup)
½ medium banana, sliced (½ cup)
1 cup diet lemon-lime soda
1 cup ice cubes
Sugar substitute equivalent to 2 teaspoons sugar

Place raspberries, banana, diet soda, ice cubes, and sugar substitute in a blender or food processor and blend until smooth. Serve in tall glasses. Makes 2 servings.

Per serving: 66 calories, 1.1 grams protein, 16.4 grams carbohydrate, 0.6 gram fat (0.1 saturated), 0 milligram cholesterol, 1 milligram sodium, 3.5 grams fiber

Shopping List

Produce
1 small daikon (white) radish
1 medium banana
¼ pound button mushrooms
¼ pound fresh snow peas

Seafood
2 (6-ounce) tuna steaks

Grocery
1 small jar five-spice powder
1 small package frozen raspberries (not in sugar syrup)
1 small can/bottle diet lemon-lime soda
1 small bottle rice vinegar
1 small bottle cracked black pepper
1 small bottle sesame oil

Staples
Garlic
30-minute quick-cooking brown rice
Sugar substitute
Fat-free, low-sodium chicken broth
Low-sodium soy sauce
Salt
Black peppercorns

Chicken with Black Bean and Corn Salsa Salad

Helpful Hints

- *Look for roasted chicken that is not marinated in honey or a barbecue sauce. These sauces usually contain sugar.*
- *This recipe calls for serving the chicken at room temperature. For a hot meal, place chicken in microwave oven on high for 2 minutes.*

Countdown

- *Start rice.*
- *Make salsa.*
- *Assemble salad.*

Shopping List

Produce

1 small bunch cilantro
2 small tomatoes

Meat

¾ pound roasted chicken breast, bones and skin removed

Grocery

1 small bottle sweet (rosso) vermouth
1 small can black beans
1 small package frozen corn kernels

Staples

30-minute quick-cooking brown rice
Canola oil
Ground cumin
Hot pepper sauce
Salt
Black peppercorns

Roasted chicken served over rice with a black bean and corn salsa dresses up roasted or rotisserie chicken breasts. They are readily available in fast food restaurants or the supermarket. ● Sweet vermouth gives this black bean and corn salsa an intriguing flavor. Use the salsa dressing in the recipe or add vermouth and cumin to a bottled low-fat vinaigrette dressing. ● Brown rice takes about 45 minutes to cook. There are several brands of quick-cooking brown rice available. Their cooking times range from 10 to 30 minutes. I find the 30-minute rice has more flavor, but any quick-cooking brown rice will work for this dinner.

¾ cup 30-minute quick-cooking brown rice
1 tablespoon plus 1 teaspoon canola oil, divided use
½ tablespoon plus 1 teaspoon sweet (rosso) vermouth
Salt and freshly ground black pepper
1 teaspoon ground cumin
Several drops hot pepper sauce
¼ cup canned black beans, rinsed and drained
¼ cup frozen corn kernels, defrosted
¾ pound roasted chicken breast, bones and skin removed
¼ cup chopped fresh cilantro
2 small tomatoes, cut into wedges

Bring a large pot with 2 to 3 quarts of water to a boil. Add rice and boil, uncovered, about 30 minutes (or follow package instructions). Drain into a sieve in the sink. Run hot water through rice and stir with a fork. Return rice to saucepan and add 1 teaspoon canola oil, 1 teaspoon vermouth, and salt and pepper to taste.

While rice cooks, mix 1 tablespoon canola oil, ½ tablespoon vermouth, cumin, hot pepper sauce, and salt and pepper to taste in a medium-size bowl. Add the black beans and corn. Toss well. Taste and add more seasoning if needed.

Spoon rice onto 2 dinner plates. Slice chicken and place on rice. Spoon salsa on top and sprinkle with cilantro.

Arrange tomatoes on the side of the dinner plates. Makes 2 servings.

Per serving: 558 calories, 32.0 grams protein, 38.4 grams carbohydrate, 18.4 grams fat (3.2 saturated), 144 milligrams cholesterol, 146 milligrams sodium, 2.6 grams fiber

Veal Piccata with Garlic Zucchini and Tomato Orzo

Tender veal scallopini are sautéed in a wine and lemon sauce for this quick meal. Garlic Zucchini and tomatoes take only minutes in the microwave oven.

Veal Piccata

2 tablespoons flour

Salt and freshly ground
   black pepper

¾ pound veal scallopini

1 teaspoon olive oil

2 tablespoons fresh lemon juice

2 tablespoons dry vermouth

¼ cup fat-free, low-sodium
   chicken broth

2 tablespoons chopped fresh
   parsley (optional)

Season flour with salt and pepper to taste. Dip veal in flour and shake off excess. Heat oil in a medium-size nonstick skillet on medium-high heat. When oil is very hot, brown veal on both sides, about 1 minute per side. Sprinkle lemon juice on top. Remove veal to a plate and cover with aluminum foil to keep warm. Raise heat to high and add vermouth and chicken broth to the skillet. Reduce the liquid by half, about 3 minutes. Add salt and pepper to taste. Spoon sauce over veal and sprinkle with parsley. Makes 2 servings.

Per serving: 424 calories, 44.2 grams protein, 12.4 grams carbohydrate, 19.1 grams fat (10.4 saturated),138 milligrams cholesterol, 177 milligrams sodium, 0.6 gram fiber

Garlic Zucchini and Tomato Orzo

⅓ cup orzo (rice-shaped pasta)

½ pound zucchini, cut into
   1-inch pieces (scant 2 cups)

1 medium tomato, cut into 1-inch
   pieces (1 cup)

2 medium garlic cloves, crushed

2 teaspoons olive oil

Salt and freshly ground
   black pepper

Bring a large pot filled with 3 to 4 quarts water to a boil. Add orzo and boil 8 minutes. Drain. Meanwhile, place zucchini, tomatoes, and garlic in a microwave-safe bowl. Cover with plastic wrap or plate and microwave on high for 3 minutes. Remove, stir, cover and microwave on high for 1 additional minute. Remove and add orzo, olive oil, and salt and pepper to taste. Toss well. Makes 2 servings.

Per serving: 157 calories, 4.5 grams protein, 23.3 grams carbohydrate, 5.1 grams fat (0.7 saturated), 0 milligram cholesterol, 6 milligrams sodium, 1.2 grams fiber

Helpful Hint

- *The vegetables can be sautéed instead of cooking them in a microwave oven. Heat the oil in a nonstick skillet, add the vegetables, cover with a lid, and cook 10 minutes.*

Countdown

- *Boil water for orzo.*
- *Prepare all ingredients.*
- *Boil orzo.*
- *While orzo boils, microwave vegetables.*
- *Sauté veal.*

Shopping List

Produce

   1 small bunch parsley
      (optional)

   ½ pound zucchini

   1 medium tomato

Meat

   ¾ pound veal scallopini

Grocery

   1 small bottle dry vermouth

   1 small box orzo

Staples

   Lemons

   Garlic

   Flour

   Olive oil

   Fat-free, low-sodium chicken
      broth

   Salt

   Black peppercorns

stage III
right carbs

Great food that's good for you too is the goal of this third phase, which is designed to become your permanent lifestyle. This is an overall balanced approach to eating. High-fiber carbohydrates are incorporated into breakfast, lunch, and dinner menus.

As with the other sections, I have organized the menus into a meal-at-a-glance chart with some easy and quick meals for midweek and those that take a little more time for the weekends. They are arranged to give variety throughout the day and over the course of the week.

Breakfast

Mediterranean Scramble on Toast with Oatmeal, and Monte Cristo Sandwich with Bran Cereal, are two of the savory breakfasts you can choose from. Try them all to add variety to your morning repertoire.

Lunch

Choose from the wide variety to fit every appetite. When you're in a hurry, grab a BLT Sandwich on Rye and Watermelon Cubes or Endive and Orange Salad with Turkey Swiss Melt and Melon Cup. When you have more time, enjoy the Blue Cheese, Roast Beef, and Pear Pasta Salad and Grapes.

Dinner

Enjoy these meals without worrying about numbers or questioning what you eat. Menus like Whiskey-Soused Salmon with Broccoli and Potatoes and Deep Dish Blueberry Cream, and Turkey Gratinée with Basil Linguine and Spiced Pineapple, will entice you to continue this low-carbohydrate, balanced style of eating.

For those days when you are really pressed for time, select Mock Hungarian Goulash with Caraway Noodles or Black Bean and Bacon Soup with Quick Brown Rice from the Super Speed Suppers section of the book.

For weekends when you have more time and want something special, try the Pan-Seared Tuna with Mango Salsa, Saffron Pilaf, and Lemon Chiffon, or Indian-Spiced Chicken with Rice and Spinach Pilaf from the Weekend Meals section of the book.

Following the Right Carb 14-Day Meal Plan, you will consume an average of 135 to 145 grams of carbohydrates per day. Carbohydrate percentage is based on carbohydrates less fiber consumed, which is the normal way of calculating carbohydrate consumption. The balance of these meals is 39 percent of calories from carbohydrates, 31 percent of calories from lean protein, 20 percent of calories from monounsaturated fat, and 6 percent of calories from saturated fat.

Right Carbs 14-Day Menu Plan at a Glance

week 1	breakfast	lunch	dinner
sunday	Ham, Red Pepper, and Onion Frittata with Bran Cereal and Juice 99	Mulligatawny Soup and Pears 107	Pan-Seared Tuna with Mango Salsa, Saffron Pilaf, and Lemon Chiffon . .162
monday	Smoked Salmon Sandwich with Oatmeal 100	BLT (Bacon, Lettuce, and Tomato) Sandwich on Rye and Watermelon Cubes 108	Creole Chicken with Quick Brown Rice and Watermelon Cubes . 139
tuesday	Strawberry Splash with Pecan and Dilled Cottage Cheese–Stuffed Endive and Bran Cereal 101	Layered Antipasto Salad and Grapefruit 109	Mahi Mahi Satay with Thai Peanut Sauce, Snow Peas and Rice, and Lychee Cup 115
wednesday	Microwave Portobello Egg Scramble with Bran Cereal 102	Blue Cheese, Roast Beef, and Pear Pasta Salad and Grapes 110	Turkey-Gratinée with Basil Linguine and Spiced Pineapple 117
thursday	Mediterranean Scramble on Toast with Oatmeal 103	Endive and Orange Salad with Turkey Swiss Melt and Melon Cup 111	Parmesan Sole with Sautéed Potato Cubes and Melon Cup 141
friday	Monte Cristo Sandwich with Bran Cereal 104	Mushroom and Sausage Soup and Tangerines . 112	Roast Pork with Chunky Strawberry Salsa and Yellow Squash and Linguine 119
saturday	Provençal Omelet with Oatmeal 105	Danish Shrimp Smørrebrød with Scandinavian Cucumber Salad and Blueberry Cup 113	Indian-Spiced Chicken with Rice and Spinach Pilaf 164

tuna tataki **p90**

antipasto salad

week 2	breakfast	lunch	dinner
sunday	Ham, Red Pepper, and Onion Frittata with Bran Cereal and Juice 99	Mulligatawny Soup and Pears 107	Whiskey-Soused Salmon with Broccoli and Potatoes and Deep Dish Blueberry Cream 121
monday	Smoked Salmon Sandwich with Oatmeal 100	BLT (Bacon, Lettuce, and Tomato) Sandwich on Rye and Watermelon Cubes 108	Roasted Pepper and Olive Snapper with Lemon-Braised Celery Hearts and Rice and Peach Crumble 123
tuesday	Strawberry Splash with Pecan and Dilled Cottage Cheese–Stuffed Endive and Bran Cereal 101	Layered Antipasto Salad and Grapefruit 109	Hawaiian Chicken with Pineapple Caesar Salad 125
wednesday	Microwave Portobello Egg Scramble with Bran Cereal 102	Blue Cheese, Roast Beef, and Pear Pasta Salad and Grapes 110	Black Bean and Bacon Soup with Quick Brown Rice 142
thursday	Mediterranean Scramble on Toast with Oatmeal 103	Endive and Orange Salad with Turkey Swiss Melt and Melon Cup 111	Mock Hungarian Goulash with Caraway Noodles 143
friday	Monte Cristo Sandwich with Bran Cereal 104	Mushroom and Sausage Soup and Tangerines . 112	Mexican Sopes (Layered Open Tortilla Sandwich) and Oranges in Cherry Coulis 127
saturday	Provençal Omelet with Oatmeal 105	Danish Shrimp Smørrebrød with Scandinavian Cucumber Salad and Blueberry Cup 113	Pork Chops with Apple Relish, Toasted Walnut Lentils, and Cranberry Applesauce 166

right carbs
breakfasts

Ham, Red Bell Pepper, and Onion Frittata with Bran Cereal and Vegetable Juice

Plump, juicy frittatas take about 10 minutes to make. They can be made ahead and eaten at room temperature. They differ from omelets. An omelet is cooked quickly over high heat, making it creamy and runny while a frittata is cooked slowly over low heat, making it firm and set. A frittata needs to be cooked on both sides. It can be flipped over in the pan, but a much easier way is to place it under a broiler for half a minute to finish cooking.

Ham, Red Bell Pepper, and Onion Frittata

Olive oil spray

1 cup sliced onion

6 ounces sliced lean ham, cut into bite-size pieces

1 medium red bell pepper, sliced (1 cup)

1 cup egg substitute

Salt and freshly ground black pepper

Preheat broiler. Heat an ovenproof medium-size nonstick skillet on medium-high heat and spray with olive oil spray. Add onion, ham, and red pepper. Cook 2 minutes. Mix egg substitute with salt and pepper to taste. Reduce heat to low and add egg mixture. Cook without browning the bottom, 10 minutes. The bottom of eggs will be set, but the top will be a little runny. Place pan under the broiler for 30 seconds to 1 minute until the top is set, but not brown. Remove and cut in half. Slide halves onto 2 plates. Makes 2 servings.

Bran Cereal

1 cup skim milk

1 cup high-fiber, no-sugar-added bran cereal

Divide ingredients between 2 cereal bowls. Makes 2 servings.

Vegetable Juice

1½ cups low-sodium, no-sugar-added tomato or V-8 juice

Divide between 2 glasses. Makes 2 servings.

Per serving: 366 calories, 38.1 grams protein, 50.6 grams carbohydrate, 7.6 grams fat (2.3 saturated), 42 milligrams cholesterol, 1178 milligrams sodium, 14.5 grams fiber

Helpful Hint

- *Be careful when removing the skillet from the broiler. The handle will be very hot and will remain hot for several minutes after it is removed. Place a pot holder or oven mitt over the handle for safety.*

Countdown

- *Preheat the broiler.*
- *Make frittata.*
- *While frittata cooks, assemble cereal.*

Shopping List

Produce

1 medium red bell pepper

Deli

6 ounces sliced lean ham

Staples

Onion

Egg substitute

Olive oil spray

Skim milk

High-fiber, no-sugar-added bran cereal

Low-sodium, no-sugar-added tomato or V-8 juice

Salt

Black peppercorns

Countdown

● *Make oatmeal.*
● *Assemble smoked salmon sandwich.*

Shopping List

Produce
  1 medium tomato

Dairy
  1 small package reduced-fat cream cheese

Seafood
  6 ounces smoked salmon

Staples
  Rye bread
  Skim milk
  Oatmeal
  Sugar substitute

Smoked Salmon Sandwich with Oatmeal

Buttery, smooth smoked salmon is a special breakfast treat.

Smoked Salmon Sandwich

2 slices rye bread
2 tablespoons reduced-fat cream cheese
6 ounces smoked salmon
½ medium tomato, sliced

Toast rye bread and spread with cream cheese. Divide smoked salmon in half and place over cream cheese on each piece of toast. Serve sandwiches with sliced tomato on the side. Makes 2 servings.

Oatmeal

1 cup oatmeal
2 cups water
1 cup skim milk
Sugar substitute equivalent to 2 teaspoons sugar (optional)

To prepare in the microwave, combine oatmeal and water together. Microwave on high for 4 minutes. Stir in milk and sugar substitute. Makes 2 servings.

   Alternatively, combine oatmeal and water in a small saucepan. Bring to a boil. Cook about 5 minutes over medium heat, stirring occasionally. Stir in milk and sugar substitute. Makes 2 servings.

Per serving: 416 calories, 28.7 grams protein, 50.7 grams carbohydrate, 11.0 grams fat (4.9 saturated), 39 milligrams cholesterol, 985 milligrams sodium, 5.6 grams fiber

Strawberry Splash with Pecan and Dilled Cottage Cheese–Stuffed Endive and Bran Cereal

Sweet strawberries flavor this quick shake that you can make and take on the run.

Strawberry Splash

1 cup soy milk
2 cups strawberries
1 teaspoon vanilla extract
Sugar substitute equivalent to
    2 teaspoons sugar

Place soy milk, strawberries, vanilla extract, and sugar substitute in a blender and blend until smooth. Divide between 2 glasses. Makes 2 servings.

Pecan and Dilled Cottage Cheese–Stuffed Endive

1 cup low-fat cottage cheese
2 tablespoons pecan pieces
2 tablespoons snipped dill or
    ½ teaspoon dried dill
1 small head Belgian endive

Mix cottage cheese, pecans, and dill together. Remove leaves from Belgian endive and fill with cottage cheese mixture. Divide between 2 plates. Makes 2 servings.

Bran Cereal

1 cup skim milk
1 cup high-fiber, no-sugar-added
    bran cereal

Divide ingredients between 2 cereal bowls. Makes 2 servings.

Per serving: 387 calories, 24.6 grams protein, 54.8 grams carbohydrate, 13.7 grams fat (2.6 saturated), 12 milligrams cholesterol, 610 milligrams sodium, 16.9 grams fiber

Helpful Hints

- Frozen or fresh strawberries can be used. Make sure frozen ones are not packed in sugar syrup.
- Any type of berries can be used.
- The stuffed endive can be made the night before and wrapped in plastic wrap.
- The easiest way to chop dill leaves is to snip them right off the stem with a scissors.
- Dried dill can be used.

Countdown

- Make shake.
- Assemble stuffed endive.

Shopping List

Produce
1 container strawberries
    (10 ounces needed)
1 small bunch fresh dill
    (or dried dill in a jar)
1 small head Belgian endive

Dairy
1 small carton soy milk
    (8 ounces needed)
1 cup low-fat cottage cheese

Grocery
1 small bottle vanilla extract
1 small package pecan pieces

Staples
Skim milk
Sugar substitute
High-fiber, no-sugar-added
    bran cereal

Microwave Portobello Egg Scramble with Bran Cereal

The earthy flavor of the portobello mushrooms and the distinctive taste of Parmesan cheese give these microwaved scrambled eggs a rich flavor.

Microwave Portobello Egg Scramble

2 slices rye bread
1/4 pound sliced portobello
   mushrooms (1 1/2 cups)
2 teaspoons olive oil
1 cup egg substitute
3 tablespoons Parmesan cheese
Pinch of ground nutmeg
Salt and freshly ground
   black pepper

Toast rye bread and place on 2 plates. Place mushrooms in a microwave-safe bowl and drizzle with olive oil. Microwave on high for 1 minute. Whisk together egg substitute, Parmesan cheese, nutmeg, and salt and pepper to taste in a bowl. Remove mushrooms from microwave and stir. Pour in egg mixture and stir. Return bowl to microwave oven and microwave on high for 1 1/2 minutes. Remove and stir. Return for another 1 minute. Divide into two portions and spoon onto toast. Makes 2 servings.

Bran Cereal

1 cup skim milk
1 cup high-fiber, no-sugar-added
   bran cereal

Divide ingredients between 2 cereal bowls. Makes 2 servings.

Per serving: 365 calories, 27.3 grams protein, 49.1 grams carbohydrate, 11.5 grams fat (3.7 saturated), 13 milligrams cholesterol, 894 milligrams sodium, 14.9 grams fiber

Helpful Hints

- Buy thinly sliced portobello or other type of mushrooms.
- Buy good-quality Parmesan cheese and ask the market to grate it for you or chop it in your food processor. Freeze extra for quick use. You can quickly spoon out what you need and leave the rest frozen.

Countdown

- Assemble cereal.
- Make eggs.

Shopping List

Produce

1 package sliced portobello
   mushrooms

Staples

Rye bread

Parmesan cheese

Egg substitute

High-fiber, no-sugar-added
   bran cereal

Olive oil

Ground nutmeg

Skim milk

Salt

Black peppercorns

Mediterranean Scramble on Toast with Oatmeal

Seasoned olives chopped and mixed with spices provide a savory accent for these quick scrambled eggs on toast.

Mediterranean Scramble on Toast

2 slices whole wheat bread
2 tablespoons olive tapenade
Olive oil spray
1 cup egg substitute
2 tablespoons grated Parmesan
    cheese
Freshly ground black pepper

Toast bread and spread with olive tapenade. Heat a small nonstick skillet on medium-high heat and spray with olive oil spray. Mix egg substitute with Parmesan cheese and pepper to taste. Pour into skillet and cook 2 to 3 minutes or until eggs are set. Divide in half and spoon on toast. Makes 2 servings.

Oatmeal

1 cup oatmeal
2 cups water
1 cup skim milk
Sugar substitute equivalent to
    2 teaspoons sugar (optional)

To prepare in the microwave, combine oatmeal and water together. Microwave on high for 4 minutes. Stir in milk and sugar substitute. Makes 2 servings.

Alternatively, combine oatmeal and water in a small saucepan. Bring to a boil. Cook about 5 minutes over medium heat, stirring occasionally. Stir in milk and sugar substitute. Makes 2 servings.

Per serving: 383 calories, 29.2 grams protein, 46.3 grams carbohydrate, 9.4 grams fat (2.8 saturated), 9 milligrams cholesterol, 700 milligrams sodium, 7 grams fiber

Helpful Hint

- Buy good-quality Parmesan cheese and ask the market to grate it for you or chop it in your food processor. Freeze extra for quick use. You can quickly spoon out what you need and leave the rest frozen.

Countdown

- Make oatmeal.
- Toast bread and spread with olive tapenade.
- Make eggs.
- Assemble scramble.

Shopping List

Grocery
1 small jar olive tapenade

Staples
Egg substitute
Parmesan cheese
Skim milk
Oatmeal
Olive oil spray
Whole wheat bread
Sugar substitute
Black peppercorns

Monte Cristo Sandwich with Bran Cereal

Helpful Hint

- *Buy turkey breast without added sugar. Honey-coated and barbecued turkey should be avoided as the glazes are sugar based.*

Countdown

- *Make sandwich.*
- *Assemble cereal.*

Shopping List

Dairy

1 small package reduced-fat Swiss cheese (2 ounces needed)

Deli

1 small package sliced turkey breast

Staples

Egg substitute
Olive oil spray
Whole wheat bread
High-fiber, no-sugar-added bran cereal
Skim milk
Salt
Black peppercorns

Here's a quick version of this old American staple made with cheese and turkey, dipped in batter and fried or baked.

Monte Cristo Sandwich

2 slices reduced-fat Swiss cheese (2 ounces)
2 slices turkey breast (1 ounce)
4 slices whole wheat bread
1 cup egg substitute
Salt and freshly ground black pepper to taste
Olive oil spray

Place 1 slice Swiss cheese and 1 slice turkey on 1 slice of bread. Cover with second slice of bread. Repeat with remaining cheese, turkey, and bread. Beat egg substitute with salt and pepper to taste. Dip closed sandwiches into egg mixture. Spray a large nonstick skillet with olive oil spray and place over medium heat. Remove sandwiches from egg mixture and place in skillet. Brown 2 minutes and turn. Cover with a lid and cook 2 minutes. Remove to 2 plates, cut sandwiches in half, and serve. Makes 2 servings.

Bran Cereal

1 cup skim milk
1 cup high-fiber, no-sugar-added bran cereal

Divide ingredients between 2 cereal bowls. Makes 2 servings.

Per serving: 372 calories, 40.2 grams protein, 52.5 grams carbohydrate, 8.9 grams fat (3.1 saturated), 27 milligrams cholesterol, 707 milligrams sodium, 19 grams fiber

Provençal Omelet with Oatmeal

The flavors of this omelet remind me of sunny Provence where thyme, parsley, peppers, and tomatoes grow abundantly in the rich soil.

Provençal Omelet

2 slices multigrain bread
Olive oil spray
½ teaspoon dried thyme
1 cup chopped fresh parsley
½ cup low-sodium, no-sugar-added tomato sauce
2 whole eggs
4 egg whites
⅛ teaspoon cayenne pepper
Salt and freshly ground black pepper

Toast bread, spray with olive oil spray, and set aside. Mix thyme, parsley, and tomato sauce together and set aside. Heat a medium-size nonstick skillet over medium-high heat. Place eggs in a bowl and stir in cayenne pepper and salt and pepper to taste. Pour the mixture into the skillet. Let the eggs set for about 30 seconds. Tip the pan and lightly move the eggs so that they all set. Cook 1½ minutes or until eggs are set. Cook a few seconds longer for firmer eggs. Spoon tomato sauce on half the omelet and fold the other half of omelet over it. Slide out of the pan by tipping the pan and holding a plate vertically against the side of the pan. Turn the pan and plate to invert the omelet onto the plate. Cut in half and serve on 2 plates with the toast. Makes 2 servings.

Oatmeal

1 cup oatmeal
2 cups water
1 cup skim milk
Sugar substitute equivalent to 2 teaspoons sugar (optional)

To prepare in the microwave, combine oatmeal and water together. Microwave on high for 4 minutes. Stir in milk and sugar substitute. Makes 2 servings.

Alternatively, combine oatmeal and water in a small saucepan. Bring to a boil. Cook about 5 minutes over medium heat, stirring occasionally. Stir in milk and sugar substitute. Makes 2 servings.

Per serving: 380 calories, 28.9 grams protein, 50.1 grams carbohydrate, 11.2 grams fat (2.6 saturated), 215 milligrams cholesterol, 373 milligrams sodium, 7.8 grams fiber

Helpful Hint

● Dried thyme is called for. If using dried spices, make sure they are less than 6 months old.

Countdown

● Make oatmeal.
● Make omelet.

Shopping List

Produce
1 small bunch parsley

Staples
Eggs (6 needed)
Multigrain bread
Olive oil spray
Low-sodium, no-sugar-added tomato sauce
Oatmeal
Dried thyme
Cayenne pepper
Skim milk
Sugar substitute
Salt
Black peppercorns

right carbs
lunches

Mulligatawny Soup and Pears

Curry powder and ginger give mulligatawny soup a pungent flavor, while chicken and freshly diced crunchy apple provide a contrast in textures. ● *Authentic curry powder is a blend of freshly ground spices and herbs such as cardamom, chilies, cinnamon, cloves, coriander, and cumin and is made fresh every day. Commercial curry powder comes in two forms: standard and Madras, the hotter one.* ● *This soup tastes great the second day. If you have time, make double the recipe and rewarm when you want to use it.*

Mulligatawny Soup

2 teaspoons canola oil

1 cup sliced onion

1 medium carrot, sliced (½ cup)

1 celery stalk, sliced (½ cup)

½ tablespoon curry powder

1 tablespoon flour

½-inch piece fresh ginger, chopped (1 tablespoon) or 1 teaspoon ground ginger

1½ cups fat-free, low-sodium chicken broth

1 cup water

½ cup light coconut milk

½ pound roasted boneless, skinless chicken breast pieces

Salt and freshly ground black pepper

1 medium apple, cored and chopped

2 tablespoons chopped fresh cilantro (optional)

4 lemon wedges

Heat oil on medium-high heat in a large nonstick saucepan. Add onion, carrot, and celery. Sauté 5 minutes. Add the curry powder, flour, and ginger and sauté about 30 seconds. Stir in chicken broth, water, and coconut milk and simmer 5 minutes. Add chicken and continue to simmer 5 minutes. Add salt and pepper to taste. Spoon into 2 bowls. Sprinkle with chopped apple and cilantro. Place lemon wedges on side. Makes 2 servings.

Per serving: 337 calories, 32.5 grams protein, 28.8 grams carbohydrate, 12.5 grams fat (3.5 saturated), 72 milligrams cholesterol, 547 milligrams sodium, 2.7 grams fiber

Pears

2 medium pears

Core and slice pears. Divide between 2 dessert plates. Makes 2 servings.

Per serving: 98 calories, 0.7 gram protein, 25.1 grams carbohydrate, 0.7 gram fat (0 saturated), 0 milligram cholesterol, 1 milligram sodium, 4.1 grams fiber

Helpful Hints

● *Curry powder can be found in the spice section of the supermarket. It loses its freshness after 2 to 3 months.*
● *The soup tastes even better as it sits. Let stand about 5 to 10 minutes and reheat if you have time.*

Countdown

● *Make soup.*
● *Assemble dessert.*

Shopping List

Produce

1 medium apple

1 small bunch fresh cilantro (optional)

1 small piece fresh ginger (or ground ginger)

2 medium pears

Meat

½ pound roasted boneless, skinless chicken breast pieces

Grocery

1 small jar/can curry powder

1 can light coconut milk (4 ounces needed)

Staples

Carrot

Celery

Lemon

Onion

Canola oil

Flour

Fat-free, low-sodium chicken broth

Salt

Black peppercorns

BLT (Bacon, Lettuce, and Tomato) Sandwich on Rye and Watermelon Cubes

This bacon, arugula, and tomato on rye bread is a modern version of the very American bacon, lettuce, and tomato sandwich.

BLT Sandwich on Rye

½ pound lean Canadian bacon, cut into 2-inch strips

2 slices rye bread

2 tablespoons reduced-fat mayonnaise

1 tablespoon frozen chopped onion, defrosted

2 cups fresh arugula, torn into bite-size pieces

1 medium tomato, sliced

Heat a medium-size nonstick skillet on medium-high heat and add bacon strips. Sauté, turning frequently, until bacon reaches desired crispness. Remove to paper towel to drain. Meanwhile, toast bread and mix mayonnaise with onion. Spread toast with mayonnaise mixture. Divide arugula into 2 servings and place on toast. Place tomato slices on arugula. Top with bacon strips. Serve as open-face sandwiches. Makes 2 servings.

Per serving: 305 calories, 26.6 grams protein, 22.5 grams carbohydrate, 11.9 grams fat (3.2 saturated), 58 milligrams cholesterol, 1321 milligrams sodium, 1.9 grams fiber

Watermelon Cubes

4 cups watermelon cubes

Divide between 2 dessert bowls. Makes 2 servings.

Per serving: 99 calories, 1.9 grams protein, 22.1 grams carbohydrate, 1.3 grams fat (0.2 saturated), 0 milligram cholesterol, 6 milligrams sodium, 1.5 grams fiber

right carbs lunches 109

Layered Antipasto Salad and Grapefruit

Shrimp, Parmesan curls, tomatoes, roasted red pepper, arugula, and lettuce form colorful layers for this antipasto salad that is topped with a flavorful Italian dressing.

Layered Antipasto Salad

2 medium tomatoes, divided use

2 tablespoons no-sugar-added oil (olive or canola) and vinegar dressing

4 cups washed, ready-to-eat Italian-style lettuce

2 medium green bell peppers, cut into rings

2 cups drained sweet pimiento, cut into strips

1 cup arugula, torn into large pieces

2 tablespoons Parmesan curls

½ pound peeled, deveined, and cooked shrimp

1 cup red onion rings

Quarter 1 tomato and place in food processor with oil and vinegar dressing. Process to make a sauce. Place lettuce in a salad bowl. Cover with a layer of sliced green pepper. Spread the pimiento on top of the green pepper and layer the arugula on top. Slice the second tomato and place it over the arugula. Make Parmesan curls by scraping a potato peeler over the cheese. Place shrimp and Parmesan curls over arugula. Sprinkle with onion rings and dressing mixture. Makes 2 servings.

Per serving: 387 calories, 33.3 grams protein, 31.8 grams carbohydrate, 13.5 grams fat (3.5 saturated), 181 milligrams cholesterol, 466 milligrams sodium, 0.4 gram fiber

Grapefruit

1 grapefruit

Cut grapefruit in half and cut around edge and between segments with a serrated knife. Place each half on a dessert plate and serve. Makes 2 servings.

Per serving: 39 calories, 0.8 gram protein, 9.9 grams carbohydrate, 0.1 gram fat (0 saturated), 0 milligram cholesterol, 0 milligram sodium, 1.3 grams fiber

Helpful Hints

- *Buy cooked, peeled shrimp from the fish counter or freezer section. Make sure they are of good quality.*
- *Look for washed, ready-to-eat lettuce that has many different-colored leaves.*
- *Any type of bowl can be used for the salad. A glass one shows off the colorful layers.*
- *Make Parmesan curls by peeling thin strips from the cheese with a potato peeler.*

Countdown

- *Prepare ingredients.*
- *Make salad.*

Shopping List

Produce

2 medium tomatoes

1 package washed, ready-to-eat Italian-style lettuce

2 medium green bell peppers

1 small bunch arugula

1 grapefruit

Seafood

½ pound peeled, deveined, and cooked shrimp

Grocery

1 large jar/can sweet pimiento

Staples

Parmesan cheese

No-sugar-added oil (olive or canola) and vinegar dressing

Red onion

Blue Cheese, Roast Beef, and Pear Pasta Salad and Grapes

Pasta tossed with sweet ripe pears, tangy blue cheese, and juicy roast beef makes this colorful and tasty lunch.

Helpful Hints

- *Domestic, crumbled blue cheese can be found in the dairy case in most supermarkets.*
- *Any short pasta can be used.*
- *Ask deli to slice the roast beef in one thick slice. It is easier to cut into cubes this way.*

Countdown

- *Boil water.*
- *While pasta cooks, prepare remaining ingredients.*

Shopping List

Produce
1 medium pear
1 small bunch grapes
1 package cherry or grape tomatoes

Dairy
1 package crumbled blue cheese

Deli
¼ pound roast beef

Grocery
1 small package whole wheat penne pasta or other short pasta (3 ounces needed)

Staples
No-sugar-added oil (olive or canola) and vinegar dressing
Salt
Black peppercorns

Blue Cheese, Roast Beef, and Pear Pasta Salad

¾ cup whole wheat penne pasta

1 medium pear, cored and sliced into 1-inch pieces

¼ pound cubed roast beef (about 1 cup)

1 cup cherry or grape tomatoes

2 tablespoons no-sugar-added oil (olive or canola) and vinegar dressing

Salt and freshly ground black pepper

3 tablespoons crumbled blue cheese

Bring a large saucepan filled with water to a boil. Add the pasta and cook 10 minutes, or according to package instructions. Do not overcook. Drain into a colander in the sink and run under cold water. Place in a bowl and add pear slices, roast beef, and tomatoes. Add dressing and salt and pepper to taste. Toss well. Sprinkle blue cheese on top. Makes 2 servings.

Per serving: 393 calories, 25.0 grams protein, 37.0 grams carbohydrate, 17.4 grams fat (5.6 saturated), 57 milligrams cholesterol, 318 milligrams sodium, 5.6 grams fiber

Grapes

2 cups grapes

Divide between 2 dessert bowls. Makes 2 servings.

Per serving: 58 calories, 0.6 gram protein, 15.8 grams carbohydrate, 0.3 gram fat (0.1 saturated), 0 milligram cholesterol, 2 milligrams sodium, 0 gram fiber

Endive and Orange Salad with Turkey Swiss Melt and Melon Cup

Belgian endive and orange segments make a colorful and quick salad. To make this ahead, assemble the salad and Turkey Swiss Melt, but add the dressing and melt the cheese on the sandwiches just before serving.

Endive and Orange Salad

2 medium heads Belgian endive
2 medium oranges
1 tablespoon pine nuts
2 tablespoons no-sugar-added oil (olive or canola) and vinegar dressing

Wipe endive with a damp paper towel. Cut 1 inch from the base end of the endive. Slice the endive crosswise and place in a bowl. Peel oranges and break or cut into segments. Add to bowl. Place pine nuts on a small foil-lined tray and toast in toaster oven or under broiler. Sprinkle on top of salad. Drizzle with dressing. Divide between 2 plates. Makes 2 servings.

Per serving: 165 calories, 1.7 grams protein, 18.3 grams carbohydrate, 8.9 grams fat (2.2 saturated), 0 milligram cholesterol, 93 milligrams sodium, 3.2 grams fiber

Turkey Swiss Melt

¼ pound sliced turkey breast
2 slices multigrain bread
1 ounce sliced reduced-fat Swiss cheese
1 medium tomato, sliced

Place turkey on bread and place sliced cheese on top. Place on foil-lined tray in toaster oven or under a broiler for 2 minutes or until cheese melts. Divide between 2 plates and place tomato slices on the side. Serve with endive salad. Makes 2 servings.

Per serving: 193 calories, 26 grams protein, 12.8 grams carbohydrate, 5.1 grams fat (1.9 saturated), 48 milligrams cholesterol, 181 milligrams sodium, 3 grams fiber

Melon Cup

3 cups melon cubes

Divide melon cubes between 2 dessert bowls. Makes 2 servings.

Per serving: 86 calories, 2.1 grams protein, 20.1 grams carbohydrate, 0.6 gram fat (0 saturated), 0 milligram cholesterol, 21 milligrams sodium, 0.8 gram fiber

Helpful Hints

- *Any type of lettuce can be used instead of the endive.*
- *Cubed fresh melon can be found in the produce section or salad bar of most supermarkets.*

Countdown

- *Preheat broiler or toaster oven.*
- *Make salad.*
- *Spoon melon into dessert bowls.*
- *Make sandwich.*

Shopping List

Produce
2 medium heads Belgian endive
1 tomato
2 medium oranges
3 cups melon cubes

Dairy
1 small package sliced, reduced-fat Swiss cheese (1 ounce needed)

Deli
¼ pound sliced turkey breast

Grocery
1 small package pine nuts
Multigrain bread

Staples
No-sugar-added oil (olive or canola) and vinegar dressing

Mushroom and Sausage Soup and Tangerines

Mushrooms and sweet sausages make this a warm and hearty lunch. Make extra and use the next day or freeze.

Mushroom and Sausage Soup

2 teaspoons olive oil

2 cups sliced onion

½ pound low-fat turkey sausage, cut into 1-inch pieces

1 pound portobello mushrooms, sliced (6 cups)

1½ cups fat-free, low-sodium chicken broth

¼ teaspoon ground nutmeg

Salt and freshly ground black pepper

Heat oil in a large saucepan on medium-high heat. Add onion and sausage. Sauté 5 minutes until onions are transparent, but do not brown. Add the mushrooms and sauté 3 minutes. Add the chicken broth and bring to a simmer. Cook 15 minutes. Add nutmeg and salt and pepper to taste. Taste and add more nutmeg, if needed. Makes 2 servings.

Per serving: 349 calories, 25.0 grams protein, 20.2 grams carbohydrate, 16.1 grams fat (3.4 saturated), 60 milligrams cholesterol, 1146 milligrams sodium, 2.5 grams fiber

Tangerines

4 tangerines

Peel and segment tangerines. Divide between 2 plates and serve. Makes 2 servings.

Per serving: 74 calories, 1 gram protein, 18.8 grams carbohydrate, 0.4 gram fat (0 saturated), 0 milligram cholesterol, 2 milligrams sodium, 3.9 grams fiber

Danish Shrimp Smørrebrød with Scandinavian Cucumber Salad and Blueberry Cup

Pretty Danish open sandwiches are attractive and good to eat too.

Danish Shrimp Smorrebrod

1 tablespoon mayonnaise

1 tablespoon freshly squeezed lemon juice

½ pound peeled, deveined, and cooked shrimp, sliced

Salt and freshly ground black pepper

2 slices rye bread

2 red lettuce leaves

½ cup diced tomato

Mix mayonnaise and lemon juice together. Add shrimp and salt and pepper to taste. Toss well. Place rye bread on 2 plates. Place a lettuce leaf on each slice. Spoon shrimp on top. Sprinkle diced tomatoes on shrimp. Makes 2 servings.

Per serving: 263 calories, 26.5 grams protein, 18.8 grams carbohydrate, 8.6 grams fat (1.4 saturated), 176 milligrams cholesterol, 423 milligrams sodium, 1.9 grams fiber

Scandinavian Cucumber Salad

Sugar substitute equivalent to 1 teaspoon sugar

6 tablespoons hot water

2 tablespoons distilled white vinegar

2 tablespoons fresh dill, chopped, or 1 teaspoon dried

1 teaspoon freshly ground black pepper

1 medium cucumber, peeled and thinly sliced (3 cups)

Dissolve the sugar substitute in hot water. When thoroughly dissolved, add vinegar, dill, and black pepper. Mix well. Pour over cucumbers and let marinate 10 minutes. Serve with sandwich. Makes 2 servings.

Per serving: 26 calories, 0.9 gram protein, 6.1 grams carbohydrate, 0.3 gram fat (0 saturated), 0 milligram cholesterol, 4 milligrams sodium, 0.9 gram fiber

Blueberry Cup

2 cups blueberries

Divide blueberries between 2 dessert bowls. Makes 2 servings.

Per serving: 82 calories, 1 gram protein, 20 grams carbohydrate, 0.5 gram fat (0 saturated), 0 milligram cholesterol, 9 milligrams sodium, 4.4 grams fiber

Helpful Hints

- *The quickest way to chop fresh dill is to snip the leaves from the stem with a scissors.*
- *Any type of leaf lettuce can be used.*
- *Slice cucumber in a food processor fitted with a thin slicing blade or thinly slice with a mandoline.*

Countdown

- *Make cucumber salad and let marinate while preparing sandwich.*
- *Make sandwich.*

Shopping List

Produce

1 medium cucumber

1 medium tomato

1 small head red leaf lettuce

1 small bunch fresh dill (or dried dill)

1 small container blueberries

Seafood

½ pound peeled, deveined, and cooked shrimp

Staples

Lemon

Rye bread

Mayonnaise

Sugar substitute

Distilled white vinegar

Salt

Black peppercorns

right carbs
dinners

Mahi Mahi Satay with Thai Peanut Sauce, Snow Peas and Rice, and Lychee Cup

Fresh fish, quickly cooked and served with a spicy peanut sauce, brings back memories of the enticing aroma of satay (Asian kebabs) cooking on small grills in the street markets of Southeast Asia. I've used peanut butter as a base for the spicy peanut sauce to shorten the preparation time. ● *If using wooden skewers, be sure to soak them in water for about 30 minutes before use. This keeps them from burning on the grill or under the broiler.* ● *The fish only needs 4 minutes to cook. Use a gas grill, which heats quickly. Otherwise, place the kebabs under a broiler or use a stove-top grill.* ● *Brown rice takes about 45 minutes to cook. There are several brands of quick-cooking brown rice available. Their cooking times range from 10 to 30 minutes. I find the 30-minute rice has more flavor, but any quick-cooking rice will work for this dinner.*

Mahi Mahi Satay with Thai Peanut Sauce

1 teaspoon canola oil

1½ tablespoons rice vinegar, divided use

1 garlic clove, bruised

Salt and freshly ground black pepper

¾ pound mahi mahi

2 (8-inch) wooden or metal skewers

2 tablespoons crunchy peanut butter

1 tablespoon low-sodium soy sauce

Sugar substitute equivalent to 2 teaspoons sugar

6 drops hot pepper sauce

Preheat grill or broiler. Mix oil, 1 tablespoon rice vinegar, and garlic together. Add salt and pepper to taste. Slice mahi mahi into strips about ½ inch thick and 4 inches long. Place in the marinade and set aside for 10 minutes, turning after 5 minutes to make sure all sides are marinated. Remove from marinade and thread the fish strips onto the skewers. I find that threading in a wave pattern allows more even cooking. Place on grill grates directly over heat. Grill 2 minutes. Turn and grill 2 minutes. Or place on a foil-lined baking sheet and broil for 2 minutes on each side.

To make the peanut sauce: In a small bowl, mix peanut butter, soy sauce, and remaining ½ tablespoon rice vinegar together until blended to a smooth consistency. Add sugar substitute and hot pepper sauce.

Serve the kebabs on a plate with a little of the sauce poured over the fish and the rest on the side for dipping. Makes 2 servings.

Per serving: 259 calories, 33.8 grams protein, 4.6 grams carbohydrate, 11.6 grams fat (2.1 saturated), 116 milligrams cholesterol, 446 milligrams sodium, 0 gram fiber

Helpful Hints

● *Any firm fish such as grouper, swordfish, or cod can be used.*

● *Rice vinegar can be bought in the Asian section of the supermarket. One-half tablespoon water mixed with ½ tablespoon distilled white vinegar may be used as a substitute.*

● *An easy way to marinate the fish is to place the marinade and fish in a self-closing plastic bag. You can easily turn the bag halfway through the marinade time to make sure all of the sides are marinated.*

Countdown

● *Preheat grill or broiler.*
● *Marinate fish.*
● *Start rice.*
● *Make sauce for fish.*
● *Grill fish.*
● *Finish rice dish.*

continues

Mahi Mahi Satay with Thai Peanut Sauce, Snow Peas and Rice, and Lychee Cup continued

Shopping List

Produce

¼ pound snow peas

Seafood

¾ pound mahi mahi

Grocery

1 small bottle rice vinegar

1 small jar crunchy peanut butter

1 small package 8-inch wooden or metal skewers

1 can lychees

Staples

Canola oil

Garlic

30-minute quick-cooking brown rice

Low-sodium soy sauce

Sugar substitute

Hot pepper sauce

Salt

Black peppercorns

Snow Peas and Rice

⅓ cup 30-minute quick-cooking brown rice

¼ pound snow peas (about 2 cups), trimmed

2 teaspoons canola oil

Salt and freshly ground black pepper

Bring a large pot with 2 to 3 quarts of water to a boil. Add the rice, stir once or twice, and let boil 25 minutes. Add the snow peas and continue to boil 2 minutes. Test a grain; rice should be cooked through, but not soft. Drain into a sieve in the sink and return to the pot. Mix in oil and salt and pepper to taste. Spoon half on each plate with kebabs. Makes 2 servings.

Per serving: 153 calories, 4.3 grams protein, 22.3 grams carbohydrate, 5.5 grams fat (0.8 saturated), 0 milligram cholesterol, 3 milligrams sodium, 2.6 grams fiber

Lychee Cup

2 cups canned, drained lychees

Divide between 2 dessert bowls. Makes 2 servings.

Per serving: 126 calories, 2 grams protein, 32 grams carbohydrate, 0.5 gram fat (0 saturated), 0 milligram cholesterol, 2 milligrams sodium, 4 grams fiber

Turkey Gratinée with Basil Linguine and Spiced Pineapple

A golden, cheesy crust tops this quick turkey and mushroom sauté. The broiled grated cheese and breadcrumb crust is called a gratin. This meal takes about 10 minutes to complete. Or you can make it ahead and then place it under the broiler just before you need it. ● The turkey breast cutlets called for in the recipe are cut about ¼ inch thick. They only need to be cooked 1 minute on each side. Watch them carefully. They become dry and tough if overdone.

Turkey Gratinée

1 teaspoon olive oil

½ pound turkey breast cutlets
    (about ¼ inch thick)

Salt and freshly ground
    black pepper

1 cup frozen chopped onion

2 medium garlic cloves, crushed

½ pound portobello mushrooms,
    sliced (about 3 cups)

1 tablespoon flour

½ cup skim milk

¼ cup plain breadcrumbs

2 tablespoons grated Parmesan
    cheese

Preheat broiler. Heat oil in a medium-size, ovenproof, nonstick skillet over medium-high heat. Brown turkey 1 minute, then turn and brown second side 1 minute. Remove to a plate and sprinkle with salt and pepper to taste. Add onion, garlic, and mushrooms to skillet and sauté 2 minutes. Add flour and continue to sauté 30 seconds. Add milk and stir 2 minutes to thicken sauce. Push mushrooms to sides of skillet and return turkey to the pan. Cover turkey with mushrooms and sprinkle with breadcrumbs and Parmesan cheese. Add salt and pepper to taste. Place under broiler for 2 minutes. Divide between 2 plates. Makes 2 servings.

> Per serving: 355 calories, 41.3 grams protein, 18.7 grams carbohydrate, 10.2 grams fat (3.5 saturated), 88 milligrams cholesterol, 312 milligrams sodium, 0 grams fiber

continues

Helpful Hints

● Buy good-quality Parmesan cheese and ask the market to grate it for you or chop it in the food processor. Freeze extra for quick use. You can quickly spoon out what you need and leave the rest frozen.

● Chicken cutlets can be substituted for turkey.

● Any green herb can be substituted for the basil.

● Fresh pineapple cubes can be found in the produce section of most supermarkets.

Countdown

● Preheat broiler.
● Make dessert.
● Boil water for pasta.
● Make turkey.
● Make pasta.

Turkey Gratinée with Basil Linguine and Spiced Pineapple continued

continued

Shopping List

Produce

1 small bunch fresh basil

½ pound sliced portobello mushrooms

1 container pineapple cubes

Meat

½ pound turkey breast cutlets (about ¼-inch thick)

Grocery

1 small jar ground allspice

¼ pound fresh linguine

1 small package plain breadcrumbs

Staples

Olive oil

Garlic

Frozen chopped onions

Skim milk

Flour

Parmesan cheese

Sugar substitute

Salt

Black peppercorns

Basil Linguine

¼ pound fresh or dried linguine

2 teaspoons olive oil

½ cup chopped fresh basil

Salt and freshly ground black pepper

Bring a large saucepan filled with 3 to 4 quarts of water to a boil. When water comes to a boil, add pasta and cook 3 minutes for fresh or 9 minutes for dried. Drain, leaving about 2 tablespoons pasta water with the pasta. Add olive oil to pasta and toss well. Add basil and salt and pepper to taste. Divide and spoon half on each plate with turkey. Makes 2 servings.

> Per serving: 219 calories, 5.8 grams protein, 35.7 grams carbohydrate, 5.4 grams fat (0.7 saturated), 0 milligram cholesterol, 1 milligram sodium, 2.1 grams fiber

Spiced Pineapple

½ teaspoon ground allspice

Sugar substitute equivalent to 2 teaspoons sugar

2 cups pineapple cubes

Mix allspice and sugar substitute together. Place pineapple cubes in a microwaveable bowl. Sprinkle spice mixture on top and toss to make sure all cubes are coated with the mixture. Place in microwave oven and microwave on high for 1 minute. Remove and divide between 2 dessert bowls. Makes 2 servings.

> Per serving: 77 calories, 0.6 gram protein, 20.2 grams carbohydrate, 0.7 gram fat (0 saturated), 0 milligram cholesterol, 1 milligram sodium, 2.4 grams fiber

Roast Pork with Chunky Strawberry Salsa, and Yellow Squash and Linguine

Pork tenderloin with chunky strawberry salsa makes a sweet and spicy dinner. Strawberries, normally used for dessert, can also be added to salads or used to make tasty condiments for cooked meats.

Roast Pork with Chunky Strawberry Salsa

¾ pound pork tenderloin

Olive oil spray

1½ teaspoons ground cumin, divided use

2 cups ripe strawberries, hulled and cut into ¼-inch pieces

Sugar substitute equivalent to 1 teaspoon sugar

¼ cup diced red onion

Several drops hot pepper sauce

1 tablespoon fresh lime juice

Salt

4 tablespoons chopped fresh cilantro (optional)

Preheat broiler. Line a baking sheet with aluminum foil and place under broiler. Trim fat from pork and cut tenderloin in half lengthwise. Spray all sides with olive oil spray. Sprinkle with 1 teaspoon ground cumin. Remove baking sheet from broiler and place tenderloin on sheet. Broil 5 minutes. Turn and cook another 5 minutes. Test pork. A meat thermometer should read 160 degrees.

While pork broils, place strawberries in a medium-size bowl and sprinkle with sugar substitute. Add onion and hot pepper sauce. Mix the remaining ½ teaspoon cumin and lime juice together and drizzle over berries. Add salt to taste. Toss well and sprinkle with cilantro. Serve pork on 2 plates with salsa on top. Makes 2 servings.

> Per serving: 333 calories, 46.7 grams protein, 13.8 grams carbohydrate, 10.1 grams fat (3.3 saturated), 146 milligrams cholesterol, 115 milligrams sodium, 2.8 grams fiber

continues

Helpful Hints

- *If you like your salsa hot, add more pepper sauce.*
- *Any type of berry can be used.*
- *Placing the pork on a preheated baking sheet helps it to cook faster.*
- *Red onion is used in both recipes. Dice at one time and divide accordingly.*
- *Any type of linguine can be used.*

Countdown

- *Preheat broiler and baking sheet.*
- *Boil water for pasta.*
- *Broil pork.*
- *Make salsa.*
- *Boil pasta and squash.*

Roast Pork with Chunky Strawberry Salsa, and Yellow Squash and Linguine continued

Shopping List

Produce

1 small package ripe
strawberries (10 ounces
needed)

1 lime

1 small bunch fresh cilantro
(optional)

1/2 pound yellow squash

Meat

3/4 pound pork tenderloin

Grocery

1/4 pound spinach linguine

Staples

Olive oil spray

Olive oil

Ground cumin

Sugar substitute

Red onions

Hot pepper sauce

Salt

Black peppercorns

Yellow Squash and Linguine

1/4 pound spinach linguine

1/2 pound yellow squash, halved
lengthwise and sliced
(about 2 cups)

1 cup diced red onion

1 tablespoon olive oil

Salt and freshly ground
black pepper

Place a large saucepan filled with 3 to 4 quarts of water on to a boil. Add the pasta and boil 5 minutes. Add the squash and onion and continue to boil 3 minutes, or until the pasta is cooked through, but firm. Drain the pasta and vegetables leaving a few tablespoons of cooking water with the pasta. Toss with the olive oil. Add salt and pepper to taste. Divide on 2 plates with roast pork. Makes 2 servings.

Per serving: 316 calories, 9.4 grams protein,
52.3 grams carbohydrate, 7.9 grams fat
(1.1 saturated), 0 milligram cholesterol, 6 milligrams
sodium, 3.5 grams fiber

Whiskey-Soused Salmon with Broccoli and Potatoes and Deep Dish Blueberry Cream

Salmon, potatoes, and whiskey combine to star in this quick dinner. Salmon is sold in thick steaks with the bone in or in thin fillets.

Whiskey-Soused Salmon

2 (6-ounce) salmon steaks
2 cups water
Pinch salt
¼ cup reduced-fat mayonnaise
1 tablespoon fresh lemon juice
1 tablespoon whiskey
Several sprigs of watercress

Rinse salmon. Bring water to a boil and add salt. Place salmon in water. Liquid should completely cover salmon. Add more water, if needed. Bring to a simmer and gently cook 5 minutes. Salmon will be opaque. Remove to 2 plates. Whisk mayonnaise, lemon juice, and whiskey together in a small bowl and spoon over salmon. Place several sprigs of watercress on the side. Makes 2 servings.

Per serving: 286 calories, 38.6 grams protein, 0.8 gram carbohydrate, 9.8 grams fat (2.3 saturated), 111 milligrams cholesterol, 114 milligrams sodium, 0 gram fiber

Broccoli and Potatoes

½ pound yellow potatoes, washed and cut into 1½-inch pieces (about 1½ cups)
2 cups broccoli florets
2 teaspoons olive oil
Salt and freshly ground black pepper
2 tablespoons snipped chives

Place potatoes in a large saucepan and cover with cold water. Cover with a lid and bring to a boil. Lower heat to medium and simmer 5 minutes. Add the broccoli florets and continue to cook, covered, 5 minutes. Drain, remove to a bowl, and toss with olive oil and salt and pepper to taste. Sprinkle with chives. Toss well. Divide and spoon onto plates with salmon. Makes 2 servings.

Per serving: 159 calories, 5.1 grams protein, 25.2 grams carbohydrate, 5.1 grams fat (0.6 saturated), 0 milligram cholesterol, 27 milligrams sodium, 3.0 grams fiber

Helpful Hints

- *The quickest way to wash watercress is to place it leaves first into a bowl of water. Leave for a minute, then lift out and shake dry.*
- *A quick way to chop chives is to cut them with a scissors.*

Countdown

- *Make dessert.*
- *Boil potatoes.*
- *Make salmon sauce.*
- *Poach salmon.*
- *Add broccoli and finish potatoes.*

continues

Whiskey-Soused Salmon with Broccoli and Potatoes and Deep Dish Blueberry Cream

continued

Shopping List

Produce
½ pound yellow potatoes
1 small package broccoli florets
1 small bunch fresh chives
1 small bunch watercress
1 small package blueberries

Dairy
1 carton nonfat vanilla yogurt

Seafood
2 (6-ounce) salmon steaks

Grocery
1 small bottle whiskey

Staples
Olive oil
Reduced-fat mayonnaise
Lemon
Cornstarch
Sugar substitute
Salt
Black peppercorns

Deep Dish Blueberry Cream

1 tablespoon cornstarch
Sugar substitute equivalent to
    2 teaspoons sugar
1 cup water
2 cups blueberries, divided use
1 cup nonfat vanilla yogurt

In a small cup, mix cornstarch and sugar substitute. Stir this mixture into water placed in a medium-size saucepan. Bring to a boil over high heat and allow to thicken. Add ⅓ cup blueberries and boil 3 minutes. Remove from heat. Divide yogurt between 2 ramekins. Spoon the remaining berries on top. Spoon sauce over berries. Refrigerate until needed. Makes 2 servings.

Per serving: 192 calories, 6.5 grams protein, 41.6 grams carbohydrate, 0.6 gram fat (0 saturated), 3 milligrams cholesterol, 104 milligrams sodium, 4.4 grams fiber

Roasted Pepper and Olive Snapper with Lemon-Braised Celery Hearts and Rice, and Peach Crumble

Fresh snapper, roasted red peppers, and Greek olives are broiled for only 8 minutes in this simple Greek meal. This quick meal was inspired by a trip to Itea, Greece, on the Gulf of Corinth. We drove to Delphi along a road bordered by an endless sea of olive trees. These amazing groves contained more than a million trees. The view over this olive carpet leading to the blue sea was spectacular. ● Brown rice takes about 45 minutes to cook. There are several brands of quick-cooking brown rice available. Their cooking times range from 10 to 30 minutes. I find the 30-minute rice has more flavor, but any quick-cooking rice will work for this dinner.

Roasted Pepper and Olive Snapper

2 (6-ounce) snapper fillets

1 tablespoon olive oil

Salt and freshly ground black
   pepper

1½ cups sliced sweet pimientos,
   drained

8 pitted black olives, cut in half

Preheat broiler. Wash fillet and pat dry with paper towel. Place in small, shallow ovenproof dish. Drizzle olive oil on top. Sprinkle with salt and pepper to taste. Place pimiento slices and olives around fish. Broil 8 minutes. If fillet is 1 inch thick, broil 10 minutes. Serve fish on 2 plates and spoon roasted peppers and olives on top. Makes 2 servings.

Per serving: 296 calories, 33.6 grams protein, 15.2 grams carbohydrate, 11.5 grams fat (1.5 saturated), 57 milligrams cholesterol, 694 milligrams sodium, 3 grams fiber

continues

Helpful Hints

- Any type of olive can be used.
- Any type of fish fillet can be used. Cook 10 minutes for each inch of thickness.

Countdown

- Preheat broiler.
- Start rice pilaf.
- Make snapper.
- While rice and snapper cook, make dessert.

Roasted Pepper and Olive Snapper with Lemon-Braised Celery Hearts and Rice, and Peach Crumble continued

Shopping List

Produce
1 bunch celery hearts
3 medium peaches

Seafood
2 (6-ounce) snapper fillets

Grocery
1 small can/jar sweet pimiento
1 container pitted black olives
(8 olives needed)
1 small package raisins

Staples
Olive oil
Butter
Flour
30-minute quick-cooking
brown rice
Fat-free, low-sodium chicken
broth
Sugar substitute
Lemon
Salt
Black peppercorns

Lemon-Braised Celery Hearts and Rice

1 cup fat-free, low-sodium
chicken broth
1 cup water
6 medium celery stalks, tender
lower sections only, cut into
2-inch pieces (about 3 cups)
1/3 cup 30-minute quick-cooking
brown rice
1 tablespoon freshly squeezed
lemon juice
2 teaspoons olive oil
1/4 cup raisins
Salt and freshly ground
black pepper

Pour chicken broth and water into a saucepan and bring to a boil on high heat. Add celery and rice and reduce heat to medium. Cover with a lid and simmer 30 minutes until stalks are tender but still firm. Drain, reserving 3 tablespoons liquid. Divide between 2 small, shallow bowls. Mix lemon juice, olive oil, and cooking liquid together and add raisins, salt and pepper to taste. Pour over rice and celery. Makes 2 servings.

> Per serving: 184 calories, 3.4 grams protein, 33.1 grams carbohydrate, 5.5 grams fat (0.8 saturated), 0 milligram cholesterol, 54 milligrams sodium, 1 gram fiber

Peach Crumble

3 medium peaches, stones
removed and sliced
2 tablespoons flour
Sugar substitute equivalent to
2 teaspoons sugar
1 tablespoon butter

Place peach slices in a bowl that can be used in a microwave oven and under a broiler. Microwave fruit on high for 2 minutes. Mix flour and sugar substitute together. Cut in butter, and rub with fingertips to make a crumbly mixture. Spoon over fruit and place under broiler 5 minutes, or until topping is golden. Divide between 2 dessert bowls. Makes 2 servings.

> Per serving: 138 calories, 1.8 grams protein, 21.6 grams carbohydrate, 5.7 grams fat (3.5 saturated), 16 milligrams cholesterol, 58 milligrams sodium, 0.8 gram fiber

Hawaiian Chicken with Pineapple Caesar Salad, and Mangoes

On a trip to Hawaii I met Chef Harold Markt who served me a Hawaiian chicken dish with a pineapple barbecue glaze. I've adapted his ideas for these recipes. Barbecue sauces can be filled with sugar. Here's one you can make with sweet flavor and not many carbs. ● Brown rice takes about 45 minutes to cook. There are several brands of quick-cooking brown rice available. Their cooking times range from 10 to 30 minutes. I find the 30-minute rice has more flavor, but any quick-cooking rice will work for this dinner.

Hawaiian Chicken

2 (6-ounce) boneless, skinless
  chicken breasts

Olive oil spray

Salt and freshly ground
  black pepper

1/4 cup no-sugar-added tomato
  pasta sauce, divided use

2 tablespoons no-sugar-added
  pineapple juice

2 teaspoons Dijon mustard

Sugar substitute equivalent to
  2 teaspoons sugar

1/2 cup 30-minute quick-cooking
  brown rice

1 teaspoon canola oil

Place chicken between 2 layers of waxed paper and flatten with a meat bat or the bottom of a heavy skillet. Spray a medium-size nonstick skillet with olive oil spray and place on medium-high heat. Brown chicken 2 minutes. Turn and brown 2 minutes. Add salt and pepper to taste to the cooked side. Lower heat to medium and spoon 1 tablespoon sauce over each piece. Cover with a lid and cook 2 minutes. A meat thermometer should read 170 degrees. Remove to 2 dinner plates and serve remaining sauce on the side. Makes 2 servings.

Per serving: 379 calories, 52.4 grams protein, 19.8 grams carbohydrate, 10.5 grams fat (2.1 saturated), 132 milligrams cholesterol, 336 milligrams sodium, 1.3 grams fiber

continues

Helpful Hints

- *Fresh pineapple cubes can be found in the produce section or salad bar of most supermarkets.*
- *Look for no-sugar-added pineapple juice.*
- *I have cooked this chicken in a skillet because it's faster and easier than lighting a grill for a midweek dinner. If you have the time, grill the chicken about 2 minutes per side and move to a cooler area of the grill. Add a spoonful of sauce to each piece and cook 2 more minutes.*
- *To cube a mango, slice off each side as close to the seed as possible. Take the mango half in your hand, skin side down. Score the fruit in a crisscross pattern through to the skin. Bend the skin backwards so that the cubes pop up. Slice the cubes away from the skin. Repeat with the other half. Score and slice any fruit left on the pit.*

Countdown

- *Make dessert and set aside.*
- *Make chicken sauce.*
- *Cook chicken.*
- *Make salad.*

Hawaiian Chicken with Pineapple Caesar Salad, and Mangoes continued

Shopping List

Produce

1 package fresh pineapple cubes (10 ounces needed)

1 small head romaine lettuce

1 small bunch chives

2 medium mangoes

Meat

2 (6-ounce) boneless, skinless chicken breasts

Grocery

1 small jar/can no-sugar-added pineapple juice

1 jar no-sugar-added Caesar dressing

Staples

Parmesan cheese

Olive oil spray

Canola oil

No-sugar-added tomato pasta sauce

Dijon mustard

30-minute quick-cooking brown rice

Sugar substitute

Salt

Black peppercorns

Pineapple Caesar Salad

2 cups pineapple cubes

4 cups romaine lettuce, torn into bite-size pieces

¼ cup snipped chives

2 tablespoons no-sugar-added Caesar dressing

2 tablespoons grated Parmesan cheese

Place pineapple cubes and lettuce in a salad bowl. Add chives and dressing. Toss well. Sprinkle the top with Parmesan cheese. Serve on 2 salad plates. Makes 2 servings.

Per serving: 162 calories, 1.5 grams protein, 20.6 grams carbohydrate, 9.7 grams fat (1.5 saturated), 18 milligrams cholesterol, 124 milligrams sodium, 2.6 grams fiber

Mangoes

2 medium mangoes cut into cubes (2 cups)

Divide mangoes between 2 dessert bowls. Makes 2 servings.

Per serving: 134 calories, 1.1 grams protein, 35.2 grams carbohydrate, 0.6 gram fat (0.1 saturated), 0 milligram cholesterol, 4 milligrams sodium, 2.2 grams fiber

Mexican Sopes (Layered Open Tortilla Sandwich) and Oranges in Cherry Coulis

On a trip to Mexico City, I watched Maricarmen Ramirez make these melt-in-your-mouth sopes. They're little corn tortillas filled with a spicy black bean spread, roasted chicken, lettuce, and cheese. Although sopes are usually served as appetizers, she mentioned that they make quick and easy supper dishes, too.

Mexican Sopes (Layered Open Tortilla Sandwich)

2 teaspoons canola oil, divided use

½ cup diced red onion, divided use

½ cup rinsed and drained canned black beans

Several drops hot pepper sauce

Salt and freshly ground black pepper

½ pound roasted or rotisserie chicken breast, skin and bones removed, shredded into bite-size pieces

4 (6-inch) corn tortillas

1 cup washed, ready-to-eat, shredded lettuce

¼ cup shredded reduced-fat Monterey Jack or Mexican-style cheese

1 cup medium-heat no-sugar-added tomato salsa

Heat 1 teaspoon oil in a large nonstick skillet on medium-high heat. Add half the diced onion and sauté until it starts to shrivel, about 3 minutes. Remove to the bowl of a food processor. Add beans, remaining 1 teaspoon oil, and hot pepper sauce and purée. If you do not have a food processor, mash the beans with a fork and mix with the onion, oil, and hot pepper sauce. If the beans are dry, add a few tablespoons of water. Add salt and pepper to taste. Set aside.

Place the same skillet over medium-low heat. Add the tortillas and warm for 30 seconds. Turn them over and spread the top of each tortilla with the black bean mixture. Sprinkle with the remaining ¼ cup onion. Layer lettuce, cheese, and chicken over each one. If tortillas do not fit in 1 skillet, cook them 2 at a time. Cover with a lid for 1 minute. Remove to 2 dinner plates. Spoon salsa on top or serve on the side. Makes 2 servings.

Per serving: 517 calories, 54.8 grams protein, 49.8 grams carbohydrate, 15.6 grams fat (4.1 saturated), 104 milligrams cholesterol, 1112 milligrams sodium, 8.0 grams fiber

continues

Helpful Hints

- *Any type of salsa can be used. Choose the heat of the salsa according to your preference.*
- *Buy washed, ready-to-eat, shredded lettuce.*
- *If all 4 tortillas don't fit into your skillet, cook them in batches.*
- *If pressed for time, use a jarred spicy black bean dip instead of making the spread in the recipe.*

Countdown

- *Make oranges and cherry coulis and set aside.*
- *Make black bean spread.*
- *Shred chicken and prepare ingredients.*
- *Make sopes.*

Mexican Sopes (Layered Open Tortilla Sandwich) and Oranges in Cherry Coulis continued

Oranges in Cherry Coulis

2 oranges
1 cup frozen sweet, dark cherries

Peel oranges and slice over a bowl to catch the juice. Defrost cherries for 1 minute in a microwave oven. Purée cherries in a food processor, adding juice from peeled oranges, or press cherries through a food mill. Spoon cherry coulis onto 2 dessert plates. Place orange slices on top. Makes 2 servings.

Per serving: 122 calories, 1.9 grams protein, 28.7 grams carbohydrate, 0.2 gram fat (0 saturated), 0 milligram cholesterol, 0 milligram sodium, 5 grams fiber

Shopping List

Produce
1 bag washed, ready-to-eat lettuce
2 oranges

Dairy
1 package shredded reduced-fat Monterey Jack or Mexican-style cheese

Meat
½ pound roasted or rotisserie chicken breast

Grocery
1 bag frozen sweet, dark cherries
4 (6-inch) corn tortillas

Staples
Canola oil
Red onion
Canned black beans
Hot pepper sauce
Medium-heat, no-sugar-added tomato salsa
Salt
Black peppercorns

pepper and olive snapper   **p123**

super speed suppers

These meals are for those nights that I haven't got time to think about dinner, but don't want to send out for something that won't fit my lifestyle guidelines. In fact they're faster and taste better than most fast food. I've based them on ingredients that I bought from the supermarket that can be assembled into a meal in 15 minutes or less.

Savory Sage Chicken with Italian Zucchini and Tomatoes is one of my favorites. It's based on roasted or rotisserie chicken that is doctored up at home. It fits the Quick Start nutritional guidelines and takes about 10 minutes to make.

I love a good, hearty bowl of soup for supper, even in the summer. The Peasant Country Soup with Herb Cheese Toast and Salad is perfect for a quick dinner. It only takes 10 minutes and fits the Which Carbs nutritional guidelines.

When I brought the Mock Hungarian Goulash and Caraway Noodles to my National Public Radio station for one of my programs, the staff all lined up for seconds. It is made in 10 minutes, uses lean roast beef from the deli, and fits the Right Carbs nutritional guidelines.

These meals have been incorporated into the 2-week menu plan for the appropriate phase. Keep some of the bottled ingredients on hand and you can throw a dinner together faster than getting into your car or calling to find a quick meal.

super speed suppers

Greek Shrimp with Feta Cheese and Romaine with Fresh Cabbage Salad

Greek feta cheese gives this shrimp dish a tangy Mediterranean flavor.

Greek Shrimp with Feta Cheese

2 teaspoons olive oil

½ cup frozen chopped onion

2 garlic cloves, crushed

1 large tomato, diced (1½ cups)

¾ pound large shrimp, shelled and deveined

½ cup crumbled feta cheese

1 teaspoon dried oregano

Salt and freshly ground black pepper

Heat olive oil in a medium-size nonstick skillet on medium-high heat and add the onion, garlic, and tomato. Sauté 3 minutes. Add shrimp and sprinkle cheese and oregano on top. Sauté 3 minutes, turning shrimp to make sure they are cooked on both sides. Remove from heat, cover with a lid, and let sit 2 minutes, or until cheese melts. Add salt and pepper to taste. Divide on 2 plates. Makes 2 servings.

Per serving: 349 calories, 41.6 grams protein, 9.6 grams carbohydrate, 14.9 grams fat (6.2 saturated), 280 milligrams cholesterol, 638 milligrams sodium, 0.9 gram fiber

Romaine and Fresh Cabbage Salad

2 cups shredded, washed, ready-to-eat cabbage

2 cups shredded, washed, ready-to-eat romaine lettuce

2 scallions, sliced (⅓ cup)

1 teaspoon dried dill

2 tablespoons no-sugar-added oil (olive or canola) and vinegar dressing

Combine cabbage, lettuce, scallions, and dill in a bowl. Add dressing and toss well. Serve on 2 chilled salad plates. Makes 2 servings.

Per serving: 104 calories, 1.4 grams protein, 6.1 grams carbohydrate, 8.7 grams fat (1.3 saturated), 0 milligram cholesterol, 91 milligrams sodium, 1.2 grams fiber

Helpful Hints

- *Shredded cabbage can be bought ready-to-eat in the produce section of the supermarket.*
- *Crumbled feta cheese can be found in the dairy section of the supermarket.*
- *Dried oregano and dill are used in this recipe. Replace dried herbs after 6 months. If they look gray and old, that's probably how they will taste.*

Countdown

- *Assemble salad.*
- *Make shrimp.*

Shopping List

Produce

1 bag shredded, washed, ready-to-eat cabbage

1 bag shredded, washed, ready-to-eat romaine lettuce

1 small bunch scallions

1 large tomato

Dairy

1 small package crumbled feta cheese

Seafood

¾ pound large shrimp

Staples

No-sugar-added oil (olive or canola) and vinegar dressing

Olive oil

Frozen chopped onion

Garlic

Dried dill

Dried oregano

Salt

Black peppercorns

Jamaican Jerk Pork with Hearts of Palm Salad

Helpful Hints

- There are several jerk seasonings, liquid and dry, available. Choose whichever one suits your taste.
- If jerk seasoning is unavailable, make your own by mixing together 1 teaspoon dried thyme, 1 teaspoon salt, ½ teaspoon allspice, ¼ teaspoon cinnamon, and a pinch of cayenne pepper.
- If you are really pressed for time, serve the jerk pork with a washed, ready-to eat salad and 2 tablespoons of no-sugar-added salad dressing instead of the hearts of palm salad.

Countdown

- Assemble salad.
- Make Jamaican Jerk Pork.

Shopping List

Produce
- 1 bag washed, ready-to-eat salad
- 1 medium cucumber
- 2 medium tomatoes

Meat
- 2 (6-ounce) boneless pork chops

Grocery
- 1 (14-ounce) can hearts of palm
- 1 small bottle jerk seasoning

Staples
- No-sugar-added oil (olive or canola) and vinegar dressing
- Canola oil

"Jerking" is an ancient Jamaican method for preserving and cooking meat. In Jamaica the men who prepare the meat and sell it to the markets are called "jerk men." They use a long process involving marinating the meat and then slowly cooking it over a pimiento (allspice) wood fire. I've captured the flavors of jerk cooking for this quick dinner by using a prepared jerk seasoning.

Jamaican Jerk Pork

2 (6-ounce) boneless pork chops, about ½-inch thick
1 tablespoon jerk seasoning
1 teaspoon canola oil

Remove fat from pork and rub with jerk seasoning. Heat oil in a medium-size nonstick skillet on medium-high heat. Add pork and brown 2 minutes. Turn and brown second side 2 minutes. Lower heat to medium and cook 2 more minutes. A meat thermometer should read 160 degrees. Move to 2 plates. Makes 2 servings.

Per serving: 287 calories, 45.3 grams protein, 1.5 grams carbohydrate, 9.8 grams fat (3.0 saturated), 146 milligrams cholesterol, 107 milligrams sodium, 0 gram fiber

Hearts of Palm Salad

1 (14-ounce) can hearts of palm (2 cups sliced)
4 cups washed, ready-to-eat salad (½ of a 10-ounce bag)
½ medium cucumber, peeled and sliced (1½ cups)
2 tablespoons no-sugar-added oil (olive or canola) and vinegar dressing
2 medium tomatoes, quartered

Drain hearts of palm and cut into 1-inch slices. Place lettuce in a bowl and add cucumber and dressing. Toss well. Add tomato wedges along edge of bowl and sprinkle hearts of palm on top. Makes 2 servings.

Per serving: 160 calories, 6.8 grams protein, 15.9 grams carbohydrate, 9.5 grams fat (1.4 saturated), 0 milligram cholesterol, 715 milligrams sodium, 4.3 grams fiber

Savory Sage Chicken with Italian Zucchini and Tomatoes

This is a tasty, 10-minute meal created by adding a quick sage and flour coating and a wine sauce to store-bought roasted chicken.

Savory Sage Chicken

1 tablespoon flour

2 teaspoons dried ground sage

Salt and freshly ground black pepper

2 (6-ounce) roasted boneless, skinless chicken breasts

1 tablespoon olive oil

¼ cup dry vermouth

¼ cup water

Mix together flour, sage, and salt and pepper to taste. Roll chicken in mixture, pressing flour into chicken on both sides. Heat a medium-size nonstick skillet on medium-high heat. Add chicken to skillet and cook 1 minute per side. Remove to a plate and raise heat to high. Add vermouth and water and reduce for 2 minutes. Pour sauce over chicken. Makes 2 servings.

Per serving: 383 calories, 54.5 grams protein, 4.1 grams carbohydrate, 14.9 grams fat (2.7 saturated), 144 milligrams cholesterol, 131 milligrams sodium, 0 gram fiber

Italian Zucchini and Tomatoes

¼ pound zucchini, sliced (2 cups)

2 medium tomatoes, cut into wedges about same size as zucchini

1 teaspoon dried oregano

2 tablespoons shredded part-skim milk mozzarella cheese

Salt and freshly ground black pepper

Place zucchini and tomatoes in a microwave-safe bowl and microwave on high for 3 minutes. Add oregano, cheese, and salt and pepper to taste. Toss well. Makes 2 servings.

Per serving: 74 calories, 6.5 grams protein, 9.6 grams carbohydrate, 2.1 grams fat (1.2 saturated), 7 milligrams cholesterol, 67 milligrams sodium, 0.9 gram fiber

Helpful Hints

- *White wine can be substituted for vermouth.*
- *Roasted boneless, skinless chicken breasts come ready packaged and can be found in the meat case of the supermarket. Or use rotisserie-roasted chicken breasts.*
- *Dried oregano and sage are used in this recipe. Replace dried herbs after 6 months. If they look gray and old, that's probably how they will taste.*

Countdown

- *Make Italian Zucchini and Tomatoes.*
- *Make Savory Sage Chicken.*

Shopping List

Produce

¼ pound zucchini
2 medium tomatoes

Dairy

1 small package shredded part-skim milk mozzarella cheese

Meat

2 (6-ounce) roasted boneless, skinless chicken breasts

Grocery

1 small bottle dry vermouth

Staples

Dried oregano
Dried ground sage
Flour
Olive oil
Salt
Black peppercorns

which carbs
super speed suppers

Swordfish in Spanish Sofrito Sauce with Yellow Rice

Onions, garlic, green peppers, and tomatoes form the basis for a Spanish sofrito sauce. The Italian sofrito is similar using chopped celery, green peppers, onion, garlic, and herbs. It's used for soups and stews. Spanish sofrito can be bought in a jar or can in many supermarkets. If difficult to find, use a thick tomato salsa instead. ● Brown rice takes about 45 minutes to cook. There are several brands of quick-cooking brown rice available. Their cooking times range from 10 to 30 minutes. The 10-minute rice is used in this dinner.

Swordfish in Spanish Sofrito Sauce

¾ pound swordfish
2 teaspoons olive oil
Salt and freshly ground
    black pepper
1 cup sofrito or thick no-sugar-
    added tomato salsa

Wash fish and pat dry with a paper towel. Heat oil in a medium-size nonstick skillet on medium-high heat and add fish. Brown for 2 minutes. Turn and brown second side 2 minutes. Salt and pepper to taste. Lower heat to medium, add sofrito, cover, and simmer 5 minutes for 1-inch-thick fish. Simmer 3 to 4 minutes for ¾-inch-thick fish. Remove to 2 plates. Makes 2 servings.

Per serving: 308 calories, 33.6 grams protein, 0 gram carbohydrate, 12.8 grams fat (2.4 saturated), 66 milligrams cholesterol, 152 milligrams sodium, 0 gram fiber

Yellow Rice

1⅓ cup water
1⅓ cup 10-minute quick-cooking
    brown rice
¼ teaspoon turmeric
¼ cup diced or sliced sweet
    pimiento, drained
1 teaspoon olive oil

Bring water to a boil in a large saucepan over high heat. Lower heat to medium-high and add rice. Cover and cook 5 minutes. Remove from heat and let stand 5 minutes. Stir in pimiento and olive oil. Add salt and pepper to taste. Divide on 2 fish plates. Makes 2 servings.

Per serving: 196 calories, 5.0 grams protein, 36.0 grams carbohydrate, 3.9 grams fat (0.6 saturated), 0 milligram cholesterol, 3 milligrams sodium, 2 grams fiber

Helpful Hints

- Any meaty fish such as halibut or tuna can be used. This meal also works well with canned tuna.
- Bijol or saffron can be used instead of the turmeric in the rice.
- Look for sofrito with 15 calories and 0.4 grams of fat per ounce.

Countdown

- Start rice.
- Make swordfish.
- Finish seasoning rice.

Shopping List

Seafood
    ¾ pound swordfish

Grocery
    1 jar/can sofrito or thick no-sugar-added tomato salsa
    1 small bottle turmeric
    1 small can/jar diced or sliced sweet pimiento

Staples
    Olive oil
    10-minute quick-cooking brown rice
    Salt
    Black peppercorns

Peasant Country Soup with Herb Cheese Toast and Salad

This warm, hearty soup can be made in about 15 minutes. It keeps well. If you have the time, make extra and freeze for another quick meal.

Peasant Country Soup

2 teaspoons olive oil
1 pound sliced button mushrooms (6 cups)
1½ cups no-sugar-added tomato pasta sauce
¾ cup fat-free, low-sodium chicken broth
¾ cup water
¾ cup cooked white navy or cannellini beans, rinsed and drained
¼ pound roasted chicken strips or pieces
Salt and freshly ground black pepper

Heat olive oil in a medium-size saucepan over high heat. Add mushrooms and sauté 1 minute. Add pasta sauce, chicken broth, water, and beans. Bring to a boil and simmer 10 minutes. Add chicken and cook 1 minute to warm through. Add salt and pepper to taste. Serve in 2 bowls. Makes 2 servings.

Per serving: 334 calories, 29.7 grams protein, 33.6 grams carbohydrate, 8.7 grams fat (1.2 saturated), 48 milligrams cholesterol, 856 milligrams sodium, 6.2 grams fiber

Herb Cheese Toast and Salad

2 slices whole wheat bread
Olive oil spray
5 tablespoons herbed goat cheese (2 ounces)
4 cups washed, ready-to-serve salad
2 tablespoons no-sugar-added oil (olive or canola) and vinegar dressing

Preheat broiler. Spray whole wheat slices with olive oil spray and spread with goat cheese. Broil 1 to 2 minutes until cheese is melted. Cut bread into 2 triangles. Place salad in a bowl and toss with dressing. Divide between 2 salad plates and place 2 toast triangles (1 slice) on the side. Serve with soup. Makes 2 servings.

Per serving: 237 calories, 10.7 grams protein, 12.6 grams carbohydrate, 18.0 grams fat (7.1 saturated), 22 milligrams cholesterol, 342 milligrams sodium, 3.3 grams fiber

Beef Teriyaki with Chinese Noodles

Juicy beef in a spicy teriyaki sauce is a traditional Japanese dish. This one can be made in minutes by buying the teriyaki sauce and the vegetables already cut for stir-fry. Many supermarkets have the meat and vegetables cut and ready to use for stir-frying in one package. Or go to the salad bar section and buy the vegetables cut up there.

Beef Teriyaki

*¾ pound sirloin steak,
    cut for stir-fry*

1 teaspoon sesame oil

1 cup sliced onion

2 garlic cloves, crushed

*¼ pound sliced mushrooms
    (1½ cups)*

¼ cup lite teriyaki sauce

Cut beef into strips, 3 inches long and ¼ inch wide, if not already cut. Heat sesame oil in a nonstick skillet or wok on high heat. Add onion, garlic, and mushrooms. Stir-fry 2 minutes. Add beef and stir-fry 1 minute. Add teriyaki sauce and continue to cook 1 minute. Cover and set aside until noodles are ready. Makes 2 servings.

Per serving: 456 calories, 63.9 grams protein, 14.2 grams carbohydrate, 17.3 grams fat (7.6 saturated), 153 milligrams cholesterol, 755 milligrams sodium, 0 gram fiber

Chinese Noodles

*1 cup fresh or steamed Chinese
    noodles or dried noodles*

1 teaspoon sesame oil

6 scallions, sliced (1 cup)

*Salt and freshly ground black
    pepper*

Bring 2 to 3 quarts of water to a boil in a large saucepan over high heat. Add noodles and cook 1 minute or according to package instructions. Drain. Add sesame oil, scallions, and salt and pepper to taste. Divide between 2 dinner plates and serve Beef Teriyaki on top.
Makes 2 servings.

Per serving: 167 calories, 5.0 grams protein, 27.6 grams carbohydrate, 4.0 grams fat (0.6 saturated), 33 milligrams cholesterol, 9 milligrams sodium, 1.1 grams fiber

Helpful Hints

- *Look for "lite" teriyaki sauce with 15 calories per tablespoon, 320 mg sodium, and 3 grams carbohydrate.*
- *Canola oil can be used instead of sesame oil.*
- *Fresh or steamed Chinese noodles can be found in the produce section of the supermarket, or dried noodles can be used.*
- *Angel-hair pasta can be substituted for the Chinese noodles.*
- *Beef top round can be used instead of sirloin.*

Countdown

- *Boil water for noodles.*
- *Make Beef Teriyaki.*
- *Make Chinese Noodles.*

Shopping List

Produce
    1 small package sliced mushrooms (¼ pound needed)
    1 small bunch scallions
    1 small package steamed Chinese noodles or dried noodles

Meat
    ¾ pound sirloin steak, cut for stir-fry

Grocery
    1 small bottle sesame oil
    1 small bottle lite teriyaki sauce

Staples
    Onion
    Garlic
    Salt
    Black peppercorns

right carbs
super speed suppers

Creole Chicken with Quick Brown Rice and Watermelon Cubes

Green pepper and onions are essential ingredients of Creole and Cajun cooking. Add some tomatoes, hot peppers and chicken and you've got a quick and easy Creole Chicken. The amount of cayenne called for in the recipe gives a mild zing to the sauce. If you like it hot, add more cayenne or serve hot pepper sauce at the table. ● Brown rice takes about 45 minutes to cook. There are several brands of quick-cooking brown rice available. Their cooking times range from 10 to 30 minutes. The 10-minute rice is used in this recipe.

Chicken Creole

1 teaspoon olive oil
1½ cup frozen chopped onion
1 cup frozen diced green pepper
4 garlic cloves, crushed
2 cups no-sugar-added chopped tomatoes
2 teaspoons dried oregano
1 tablespoon Worcestershire sauce
⅛ teaspoon cayenne pepper
¾ pound roasted boneless, skinless chicken breast, cut into 1-inch cubes
Salt and freshly ground black pepper
Hot pepper sauce

Heat olive oil in a medium-size nonstick skillet on medium-high heat and add onion, green pepper, and garlic. Sauté 2 minutes. Add tomatoes, oregano, Worcestershire sauce, cayenne pepper, and chicken to pan. Simmer 3 minutes. Add salt and pepper to taste. Cover dish. When rice is ready, divide it on 2 plates, spoon chicken and sauce over rice and pass the hot pepper sauce. Makes 2 servings.

Per serving: 436 calories, 59.1 grams protein, 28.1 grams carbohydrate, 10.5 grams fat (2.2 saturated), 144 milligrams cholesterol, 411 milligrams sodium, 4.6 grams fiber

Quick Brown Rice

1 cup 10-minute quick-cooking brown rice
1 cup water
Salt and freshly ground black pepper

Bring water to a boil in a large saucepan over high heat and add rice. Boil 5 minutes. Cover with a lid and let stand 5 minutes, or follow package instructions. Fluff with a fork and add salt and pepper to taste. Makes 2 servings.

Per serving: 128 calories, 3.8 grams protein, 26.3 grams carbohydrate, 1.3 grams fat (0.2 saturated), 0 milligram cholesterol, 0 milligram sodium, 1.5 grams fiber

continues

Helpful Hints

● Look for roasted chicken breasts that have not been cooked in a honey, sugar, or barbecue sauce.
● Dried oregano is used in this recipe. Replace dried herbs after 6 months. If they look gray and old, that's probably how they will taste.
● Fresh watermelon cubes can be found in the produce section or salad bar of most supermarkets.

Countdown

● Boil water for rice.
● Make chicken dish and cover to keep warm.
● Make rice.
● Assemble the watermelon cubes.

Creole Chicken with Quick Brown Rice and Watermelon Cubes continued

Shopping List

Produce

2 cups watermelon cubes

Meat

¾ pound roasted boneless, skinless chicken breast

Grocery

1 can/jar no-sugar-added chopped tomatoes (16 ounces needed)

Staples

Frozen chopped onion

Frozen diced green pepper

Garlic

Cayenne pepper

Dried oregano

Worcestershire sauce

Hot pepper sauce

10-minute, quick-cooking brown rice

Olive oil

Salt

Black peppercorns

Watermelon Cubes

2 cups watermelon cubes

Divide between 2 dessert bowls. Makes 2 servings.

Per serving: 49 calories, 1 gram protein, 11.1 grams carbohydrate, 0.7 grams fat (0.1 saturated), 0 milligrams cholesterol, 3 milligrams sodium, 0.8 grams fiber

Parmesan Sole with Sautéed Potato Cubes and Melon Cup

Fish is the original fast food. It takes only minutes to cook. For this quick meal, grated Parmesan cheese and breadcrumbs top the sole. This entire meal can be put together in 15 minutes.

Parmesan Sole

Olive oil spray
¾ pound sole fillet (½ inch thick)
2 teaspoons olive oil
2 tablespoons Italian seasoned breadcrumbs
2 tablespoons freshly grated Parmesan cheese
Salt and freshly ground black pepper
2 small tomatoes, sliced

Preheat broiler. Line a baking tray with aluminum foil and spray with olive oil spray. Rinse fish and pat dry. Place on tray and brush with 1 teaspoon olive oil. Broil 5 minutes. Mix together breadcrumbs, Parmesan cheese, remaining oil, and salt and pepper to taste. Remove sole from broiler and place tomato slices over fish. Spread breadcrumb mixture evenly over fish. Broil 2 minutes. Remove and serve. Makes 2 servings.

Per serving: 287 calories, 38.1 grams protein, 6.8 grams carbohydrate, 11.5 grams fat (3.4 saturated), 64 milligrams cholesterol, 300 milligrams sodium, 0 gram fiber

Potato Cubes

¾ pound yellow or red potatoes
2 teaspoons olive oil
Salt and freshly ground black pepper

Wash, but do not peel, potatoes. Cut into 1-inch cubes. Place in microwave-safe bowl and cover with plastic wrap or a plate. Microwave on high for 5 minutes. Remove and let stand, covered, 1 minute. Remove cover carefully, because the steam will be very hot. Add olive oil and salt and pepper to taste. Toss well. Makes 2 servings.

Per serving: 180 calories, 3.5 grams protein, 30.6 grams carbohydrate, 4.7 grams fat (0.6 saturated), 0 milligram cholesterol, 11 milligrams sodium, 2.7 grams fiber

Melon Cubes

3 cups melon cubes

Divide between 2 dessert bowls. Makes 2 servings.

Per serving: 86 calories, 2.1 grams protein, 20.1 grams carbohydrate, 0.6 gram fat (0 saturated), 0 milligrams cholesterol, 21 milligrams sodium, 0.8 gram fiber

Helpful Hints

- Any type of delicate whitefish fillet can be used such as snapper or flounder.
- Fresh melon cubes can be found in the produce section or salad bar of most supermarkets.

Countdown

- Preheat broiler.
- Make potato cubes.
- Make Parmesan Sole.
- Assemble watermelon cubes.

Shopping List

Produce
¾ pound yellow or red potatoes
2 small tomatoes
1 container melon cubes (about 1 pound)

Seafood
¾ pound sole fillet

Grocery
Italian seasoned breadcrumbs

Staples
Olive oil spray
Olive oil
Parmesan cheese
Salt
Black peppercorns

Black Bean and Bacon Soup with Quick Brown Rice

Helpful Hints

- If you like your black bean soup thick, remove about 1 cup of beans from the soup after it is cooked and purée them in a food processor. Stir the purée into the soup.
- Any type of hard grating cheese can be used.
- Brown rice takes about 45 minutes to cook. There are several brands of quick-cooking brown rice available. Their cooking times range from 10 to 30 minutes. Use the 10-minute rice for this dinner.

Countdown

- Make rice.
- Make soup.

Shopping List

Deli
- 6 ounces lean Canadian bacon
- 1 small package Manchego cheese

Staples
- 10-minute, quick-cooking brown rice
- Olive oil
- Frozen diced green pepper
- Frozen chopped onion
- Canned black beans (8 ounces needed)
- Fat-free, low-sodium chicken broth
- Chili powder
- Salt
- Black peppercorns

This meal fits the nutritional guidelines for the Right Carbs phase. ● This hearty black bean soup makes a quick one-pot dinner. Manchego is a flavorful, semi-firm Spanish cheese made from sheep's milk.

Black Bean and Bacon Soup

1 tablespoon olive oil
6 ounces lean Canadian bacon, cut into 2-inch strips
1 cup frozen diced green pepper
1 cup frozen chopped onion
2 cups rinsed and drained black beans
1 cup fat-free, low-sodium chicken broth
1 cup water
1 tablespoon chili powder
Salt and freshly ground black pepper
1/2 cup grated Manchego cheese

Heat olive oil in a large saucepan on medium-high heat. Add the Canadian bacon, green pepper, and onion. Sauté 1 minute. Add beans, chicken broth, water, and chili powder. Bring to a simmer and cook 5 minutes. Add salt and pepper to taste. Sprinkle cheese on top. To serve, divide rice between 2 soup bowls and spoon soup on top. Makes 2 servings.

Per serving: 555 calories, 41.8 grams protein, 54.0 grams carbohydrate, 19.4 grams fat (6.9 saturated), 65 milligrams cholesterol, 1100 milligrams sodium, 7.2 grams fiber

Quick Brown Rice

2/3 cup 10-minute quick-cooking brown rice
2/3 cup water
Salt and freshly ground black pepper

Bring water to a boil in a large saucepan over high heat and add rice. Boil 5 minutes. Cover with a lid and let stand 5 minutes, or follow package instructions. Fluff with a fork and add salt and pepper to taste. Makes 2 servings.

Per serving: 85 calories, 2.5 grams protein, 17.5 grams carbohydrate, 0.8 gram fat (0.2 saturated), 0 milligram cholesterol, 0 milligram sodium, 1 gram fiber

Mock Hungarian Goulash with Caraway Noodles

Succulent beef in a tomato sauce flavored with onion, green pepper, and paprika is the basis for Hungarian Goulash. I've shortened this recipe by using good-quality, lean deli roast beef and called it Mock Hungarian Goulash. ● The secret to a good Hungarian Goulash is good Hungarian paprika. Paprika is the Hungarian name for both sweet pepper and the powder made from it. Ordinary paprika comes in varying degrees of flavor—from pungent to virtually tasteless. True Hungarian paprika may be hot or mild and can be found in most supermarkets.

Mock Hungarian Goulash

1 teaspoon olive oil

½ cup frozen chopped onion

1 cup frozen diced green pepper

1 cup sliced portobello
  mushrooms

1 tablespoon Hungarian paprika or
  1½ tablespoons ordinary
  paprika

1 cup low-sodium, no-sugar-
  added tomato sauce

6 ounces thick sliced lean deli
  roast beef, cut into ½-inch-wide
  strips

Salt and freshly ground
  black pepper

2 tablespoons reduced-fat
  sour cream

2 medium tomatoes,
  cut into wedges

Heat oil in a medium-size nonstick skillet on medium-high heat and add onion, green pepper, and mushrooms. Sauté 1 minute. Sprinkle paprika over vegetables and sauté 3 minutes. Add tomato sauce and simmer 1 minute. Add roast beef and salt and pepper to taste. Remove from heat and serve over noodles. Spoon sour cream on top and arrange tomatoes on the side. Makes 2 servings.

Per serving: 311 calories, 31.0 grams protein, 21.3 grams carbohydrate, 10.8 grams fat (4.0 saturated), 77 milligrams cholesterol, 100 milligrams sodium, 1.5 grams fiber

continues

Helpful Hints

● Look for thinly sliced mushrooms in the produce section or salad bar of the supermarket. Any type of sliced mushrooms can be used.

● If Hungarian paprika is unavailable, use regular paprika. If you have it on hand, make sure it is fresh. If your paprika is older than 6 months, it's time for a fresh bottle.

Countdown

● Boil water for noodles.
● Make goulash.
● Make noodles.
● Assemble meal.

Mock Hungarian Goulash with Caraway Noodles continued

Shopping List

Produce

1 small package sliced
portobello mushrooms
(about 1½ ounces needed)

2 medium tomatoes

Dairy

1 small carton reduced-fat
sour cream

Deli

6 ounces thick-sliced lean deli
roast beef

Grocery

1 container Hungarian paprika
or ordinary paprika

1 small bottle caraway seeds

¼ pound flat egg noodles

Staples

Olive oil

Frozen chopped onion

Frozen diced green pepper

Low-sodium, no-sugar-added
tomato sauce

Salt

Black peppercorns

Caraway Noodles

¼ pound flat egg noodles
2 teaspoons olive oil
1 tablespoon caraway seeds
Salt and freshly ground
black pepper

Bring 2 to 3 quarts of water to a boil in a large saucepan over high heat. Add the noodles and boil 3 to 4 minutes or according to package instructions. Drain, leaving about 2 tablespoons water with the noodles. Toss with oil and caraway seeds. Add salt and pepper to taste. Divide between 2 plates. Makes 2 servings.

Per serving: 228 calories, 6.7 grams protein,
34.8 grams carbohydrate, 6.6 grams fat
(1.0 saturated), 46 milligrams cholesterol,
10 milligrams sodium, 1.5 grams fiber

creole chicken   p139

p157 chicken and walnuts

weekend meals

By noon on Friday, I'm already looking forward to relaxing on the weekend. I also look forward to meals that are a little extra special, but I don't want to spend all day preparing them.

The recipes in this section are still quick and easy, but take a few extra minutes of preparation or contain special ingredients that you may not think of for weeknight dinners. I've made dinner parties using these meals without telling anyone they were low-carb. No one knew and the only question asked was, "Could I have the recipe?"

Garlic-Stuffed Steak with Linguine and Asparagus is a fun weekend meal with a dessert that meets the guidelines for the Quick Start section.

Chicken and Walnuts in Lettuce Puffs with Sweet and Sour Cabbage and Oranges is a dinner with an Asian theme that fits the Which Carb Meal Plan.

Pan-Seared Tuna with Mango Salsa, Saffron Pilaf, and Lemon Chiffon is a delightful blend of fusion flavors and styles that fit the Right Carbs phase.

All of the weekend meals in this section are incorporated in the 2-week meal plan for the appropriate phase.

quick start
weekend meals

Dijon Chicken with Crunchy Couscous

A tangy mustard sauce gently coats these chicken breasts. The couscous is made with lettuce, giving a crunchy texture to the couscous. We don't often think of cooking lettuce, but the French braise lettuce and use it to make soup.

Dijon Chicken

2 (6-ounce) boneless, skinless
    chicken breasts
Olive oil spray
Freshly ground black pepper
½ cup dry vermouth
2 tablespoons Dijon mustard
2 tablespoons coarse-grain
    mustard
1 tablespoon whipping cream

Place chicken between 2 pieces of waxed paper and flatten with a meat bat or the bottom of a heavy skillet to ½ inch thick. Heat a medium-size nonstick skillet on medium-high heat and spray with olive oil spray. Brown chicken 2 minutes, then turn and brown second side 2 minutes. Add pepper to taste to the cooked side. Remove chicken to a plate and add vermouth to the skillet. Cook 30 seconds, then add the two mustards and stir to blend, about 30 seconds. Return chicken to the skillet and cook 1 minute. Remove skillet from the heat and stir in the cream. Sprinkle pepper to taste. Serve chicken on 2 dinner plates with the sauce spooned on top. Makes 2 servings.

Per serving: 400 calories, 55.4 grams protein, 3.7 grams carbohydrate, 14.2 grams fat (4.2 saturated), 155 milligrams cholesterol, 859 milligrams sodium, 0 gram fiber

Crunchy Couscous

1 cup water
⅔ cup precooked couscous
2 cups shredded iceberg lettuce
Salt and freshly ground black
    pepper
2 tablespoons slivered almonds
Several sprigs watercress,
    for garnish

Bring water to a boil in a medium saucepan on high heat. Add couscous and lettuce. Remove from the heat, cover, and let sit 5 minutes. Fluff couscous with a fork and add almonds and salt and pepper to taste. Divide on dinner plate with chicken. Arrange sprigs of watercress on the side. Makes 2 servings.

Per serving: 146 calories, 5.8 grams protein, 18.4 grams carbohydrate, 6.2 grams fat (0.4 saturated), 0 milligram cholesterol, 12 milligrams sodium, 2.1 grams fiber

Helpful Hints

- Four tablespoons of Dijon mustard can be used instead of the combination of Dijon and coarse-grain mustard.
- Any type of berry can be used for the dessert.
- Look for low-fat frozen yogurt with 240 calories, 6 grams fat, and 40 grams carbs per cup. Some brands have fewer calories and less fat and carbs. Use whichever one you can find.

Countdown

- Make couscous.
- Make chicken while couscous sits.
- Assemble chicken with sauce, couscous, and garnish.

Shopping List

Produce
1 small head iceberg lettuce
1 bunch watercress

Dairy
1 small carton whipping cream

Meat
2 (6-ounce) boneless, skinless chicken breasts

Grocery
1 small bottle dry vermouth
1 small jar coarse-grain mustard
1 small package couscous
1 small package slivered almonds

Staples
Olive oil spray
Dijon mustard
Salt
Black peppercorns

Garlic-Stuffed Steak with Linguine and Asparagus

Garlic and parsley stuffed into a juicy steak make a perfect quick meal for the weekend.
- *The garlic cloves for this stuffing are blanched first and then chopped with fresh parsley to make a simple stuffing. Blanching gives the garlic a mild, sweet flavor. The water used for blanching the garlic has a wonderful flavor, so I add it to the water for cooking the pasta.*
- *The asparagus is added to the boiling pasta for the last 5 minutes. This saves time and an extra pot to wash. If using fresh pasta, the cooking time will be about 3 to 4 minutes. Add the asparagus first and then the fresh pasta.*

Garlic-Stuffed Steak

5 garlic cloves, peeled
3/4 pound strip steak
1/2 cup chopped parsley
Salt and freshly ground
    black pepper
1 teaspoon olive oil

Place whole, peeled garlic cloves in a large saucepan and cover with cold water. Bring to a boil and scoop out garlic cloves with a strainer. Fill the saucepan with more cold water and bring to a boil for the linguine side dish.

Remove fat from steak and make slits about 1 inch apart on top and bottom to form pockets for the stuffing. The slits should be about 1/2 inch deep and cover the width of the steak.

Chop the garlic and parsley together. Add salt and pepper to taste. With the tip of a knife or a small spoon, stuff the slits in the steak using about half the parsley mixture. Set the rest of the stuffing aside. Heat a medium-size nonstick skillet on medium-high heat and add the stuffed steak. Sauté 5 minutes. Turn and sauté 5 minutes for rare. A meat thermometer should read 145 degrees. Cook 1 to 2 minutes longer for medium-rare or longer, if you prefer your meat more well cooked. Salt and pepper the cooked sides of steak. Remove from skillet to a cutting board and add the olive oil to the skillet. Add remaining stuffing and sauté 1 to 2 minutes. Cut the steak into 1-inch slices and divide between 2 dinner plates. Spoon sautéed stuffing on top of slices. Makes 2 servings.

Per serving: 397 calories, 61.5 grams protein, 3.6 grams carbohydrate, 17.1 grams fat (7.5 saturated), 153 milligrams cholesterol, 119 milligrams sodium, 0 gram fiber

continues

Linguine and Asparagus

2 ounces whole wheat linguine
  (¾ cup uncooked)

¼ pound asparagus
  (about 1 cup sliced)

2 teaspoons olive oil

Salt and freshly ground black
  pepper

2 tablespoons grated Parmesan
  cheese

Bring a large saucepan with 2 to 3 quarts of water to a boil on high heat, using the garlic water from the stuffed steak recipe and additional water to make 2 to 3 quarts. Add the linguine and boil 5 minutes. Cut 1 inch from bottoms of asparagus and cut the asparagus spears into 1 inch slices. Add the asparagus to the linguine and continue to boil 5 minutes. Remove 2 tablespoons of the water and place in a large bowl. Drain the linguine and asparagus. Add olive oil and salt and pepper to taste to the water in the bowl. Add the drained pasta and toss well. Divide on plates with steak. Sprinkle with Parmesan cheese. Makes 2 servings.

Per serving: 179 calories, 8.7 grams protein, 20.4 grams carbohydrate, 7.9 grams fat (2.5 saturated), 7 milligrams cholesterol, 180 milligrams sodium, 4.3 grams fiber

Shopping List

Produce
  ¼ pound asparagus
  1 small bunch parsley

Meat
  ¾ pound strip steak

Grocery
  1 small package whole wheat
    linguine (2 ounces needed)

Staples
  Garlic
  Olive oil
  Parmesan cheese
  Salt
  Black peppercorns

Veal Saltimbocca with Parmesan Zucchini and Italian Salad

Helpful Hints

- Ask your meat department to flatten veal for you. Or flatten it with the bottom of a heavy frying pan or meat bat.
- Veal may come in smaller pieces. Fill and roll in same manner, dividing filling among the pieces.

Countdown

- Make Parmesan Zucchini and Italian Salad
- Make Veal Saltimbocca.

Saltimbocca means "jump in mouth," which perfectly describes this dish. Fresh veal scallopini, an Italian staple, needs only a few minutes cooking in a light wine sauce to flavor it.

Veal Saltimbocca

2 (3-ounce) veal cutlets
Salt and freshly ground
   black pepper
2 thin slices lean ham (1 ounce)
4 small fresh sage leaves
2 teaspoons olive oil
¼ cup dry white wine
2 tablespoons water

Place veal on cutting board and salt and pepper the side facing up. Lay one piece of ham on each piece. Cut each sage leaf into strips and place evenly on ham. Roll up from the narrow end and secure with a wooden toothpick.

Heat the oil in a medium-size nonstick skillet on medium-high heat. Add the veal rollups and sauté until brown on all sides, about 2 minutes per side. Add the wine, lower heat to medium, and gently simmer 5 minutes.

Remove veal to 2 dinner plates and remove the toothpicks. Add water to skillet and reduce the liquid over high heat for 1 minute. Add salt and pepper to taste. Spoon sauce over veal. Makes 2 servings.

Per serving: 263 calories, 25.2 grams protein, 0.4 gram carbohydrate, 14.3 grams fat(6.3 saturated), 82 milligrams cholesterol, 178 milligrams sodium, 0 gram fiber

continues

Parmesan Zucchini

2 tablespoons grated Parmesan
    cheese
⅓ cup plain breadcrumbs
½ pound zucchini, cut into
    ½-inch slices
1 teaspoon olive oil
Salt and freshly ground
    black pepper

Preheat broiler. Mix Parmesan cheese and breadcrumbs together and set aside. Place zucchini slices in a shallow, microwave-safe bowl, cover, and microwave on high for 3 minutes. (Or bring a small saucepan filled with water to a boil. Add zucchini and boil 3 to 4 minutes. Drain and place in shallow baking dish.) Drizzle olive oil and salt and pepper to taste over zucchini. Sprinkle with Parmesan mixture and place under broiler for 1 to 2 minutes or until topping is golden.
Makes 2 servings.

> Per serving: 128 calories, 5.2 grams protein, 12.2 grams carbohydrate, 5.8 grams fat (2.3 saturated), 7 milligrams cholesterol, 281 milligrams sodium, 0.8 gram fiber

Italian Salad

4 cups washed, ready-to-eat
    Italian-style salad
2 tablespoons no-sugar-added oil
    (olive or canola) and balsamic
    vinegar dressing

Place salad in a bowl and add dressing. Toss well. Makes 2 servings.

> Per serving: 87 calories, 0.8 gram protein, 2.3 grams carbohydrate, 8.5 grams fat (1.3 saturated), 0 milligram cholesterol, 83 milligrams sodium, 0.4 gram fiber

Shopping List

Produce
    1 bag washed, ready-to-eat
        Italian-style salad
    ½ pound zucchini
    1 small bunch fresh sage
        leaves

Deli
    1 small package lean ham
        (1 ounce needed)

Meat
    2 (3-ounce) veal cutlets

Grocery
    1 small bottle dry white wine
    1 small package plain
        breadcrumbs
    1 bottle no-sugar-added oil
        (olive or canola) and
        balsamic vinegar dressing

Staples
    Parmesan cheese
    Olive oil
    Salt
    Black peppercorns

which carbs
weekend meals

Snapper Côte d'Azur with Salade de Provence and Pears with Raspberry Coulis

Sunny Provence with its abundance of fresh vegetables and herbs has a cuisine that is fragrant and simple. ● The snapper recipe calls for one uncommon vegetable—fennel. It is bulbous, with wide, celery-like stems and bright green feathery leaves. It has a very light licorice flavor. I use the feathery leaves as a garnish. ● Pernod, a licorice-flavored liqueur, is a perfect partner with fennel. You can buy small miniature Pernod bottles (splits) or use a dry vermouth instead.

Snapper Côte d'Azur

¾ pound red snapper fillets (about
   ½ inch thick)

1 small bulb fennel, sliced
   (about 2 cups)

2 teaspoons olive oil

2 medium garlic cloves, crushed

¼ cup Pernod

2 tablespoons whipping cream

Salt and freshly ground
   black pepper

Rinse the fish and pat dry with a paper towel. Remove top of fennel leaving only white bulb; wash feathery leaves and chop 2 tablespoons of leaves. Reserve some fennel ferns for garnish. Wash the fennel bulb and thinly slice. Heat the oil in a medium-size nonstick skillet over medium-high heat. Add fennel slices and leaves and garlic. Sauté 3 minutes. Add fish and cook for 4 minutes per side. Remove fish to a plate and cover with aluminum foil to keep warm.

Add Pernod and reduce for 1 minute over high heat. Stir in cream and salt and pepper to taste. Spoon sauce with sliced fennel over snapper and sprinkle fennel ferns on top. Place on 2 dinner plates. Makes 2 servings.

Per serving: 374 calories, 35.3 grams protein, 1.5 grams carbohydrate, 12.8 grams fat (4.5 saturated), 83 milligrams cholesterol, 114 milligrams sodium, 0 gram fiber

Salade de Provence (French Provincial Salad)

1 tablespoon red wine vinegar

1 teaspoon Dijon mustard

1 teaspoon olive oil

¼ cup nonfat plain yogurt

½ small head soft Bibb lettuce,
   washed and dried

4 radishes, sliced

1 small green bell pepper, sliced

6 pitted green olives

2 small whole wheat rolls

Preheat oven to 350 degrees. Mix vinegar and mustard together in a salad bowl. Add oil and mix well. Blend in yogurt. Add lettuce, radishes, green pepper, and olives. Toss well. Warm rolls in oven while fish cooks. Makes 2 servings.

Per serving: 145 calories, 7.9 grams protein, 20.8 grams carbohydrate, 5.2 grams fat (0.5 saturated), 1 milligram cholesterol, 493 milligrams sodium, 3.6 grams fiber

Helpful Hints

- Any type of light whitefish can be used. Cook the fish 10 minutes per inch of thickness.
- Any type of lettuce can be used for the salad.
- Two tablespoons of a no-sugar-added dressing can be used for the salad instead of dressing in recipe.
- Cut off fennel stalks and slice, using the thin slicing blade of a food processor or mandoline.
- A quick way to chop the fennel leaves is to snip them off the stalk with a scissors.

Countdown

- Make Pears with Raspberry Coulis.
- Preheat oven or toaster oven to warm rolls.
- Make salad.
- Heat rolls.
- Make fish.

continues

Snapper Côte d'Azur with Salade de Provence and Pears with Raspberry Coulis

continued

Shopping List

Produce

1 small bulb fennel

1 small head Bibb lettuce

1 small bunch radishes

1 small green bell pepper

2 medium pears

1 small package raspberries

Dairy

1 small container nonfat plain yogurt

1 small carton whipping cream

Seafood

¾ pound red snapper fillets

Grocery

1 small container pitted green olives (6 needed)

1 small package whole wheat rolls (2 needed)

1 miniature Pernod bottle

Staples

Red wine vinegar

Dijon mustard

Olive oil

Garlic

Sugar substitute

Salt

Black peppercorns

Pears with Raspberry Coulis

1 cup raspberries

Sugar substitute equivalent to 2 teaspoons sugar

2 medium pears

Place raspberries and sugar substitute in the bowl of a food processor and process until smooth. If you do not have a food processor, press berries through a sieve. Spoon sauce onto 2 dessert plates. Cut pears in half and remove cores. Cut into slices and place on sauce. Makes 2 servings.

Per serving: 129 calories, 1.3 grams protein, 32.7 grams carbohydrate, 1.1 grams fat (0 saturated), 0 milligram cholesterol, 1 milligram sodium, 7 grams fiber

Adobo-Rubbed Cowboy Steak with Jalapeño Rice

Texas cowboys working near the Rio Grande border loved their cowboy steaks flavored with Mexican spices. The spice mixture forms a crisp coating over the steak, keeping the meat juicy with a burst of flavor. ● *Brown rice takes about 45 minutes to cook. There are several brands of quick-cooking brown rice available. Their cooking times range from 10 to 30 minutes. I find the 30-minute rice has more flavor, but any quick-cooking rice will work for this dinner.*

Adobo-Rubbed Cowboy Steak

1 teaspoon ground cumin
1 teaspoon ground ginger
1 teaspoon dried thyme
⅛ teaspoon cayenne pepper
2 medium garlic cloves, crushed
¾ pound sirloin steak (skirt, flank, or strip can be used), fat removed
Olive oil spray
Salt

Preheat broiler. Line a baking tray with aluminum foil. Combine cumin, ginger, thyme, cayenne, and garlic in a bowl. Remove fat from steak. Spoon spice mixture over both sides of steak and press in with the back of a spoon. Spray both sides of steak with olive oil spray. Let sit 15 minutes while you prepare the rice.

Place steak on baking tray in broiler. Broil 5 minutes. Turn and broil 4 to 5 minutes for medium-rare. A meat thermometer should read 145 degrees for rare. Broil a minute longer for a steak about 1 inch thick. Cook longer if you prefer your meat more well done. Sprinkle with salt to taste. Divide and place on 2 dinner plates. Makes 2 servings.

Per serving: 350 calories, 55.8 grams protein, 1.2 grams carbohydrate, 15.5 grams fat (7.2 saturated), 140 milligrams cholesterol, 104 milligrams sodium, 0 gram fiber

continues

Helpful Hints

● Any type of steak can be used.
● Dried thyme is used in this recipe. Replace dried herbs after 6 months. If they look gray and old, that's probably how they will taste.

Countdown

● Preheat broiler and place foil-lined baking sheet on top shelf.
● Start rice.
● Mix rub ingredients and marinate steak.
● Prepare remaining ingredients.
● Broil steak.
● Finish rice.

Adobo-Rubbed Cowboy Steak with Jalapeño Rice continued

Shopping List

Produce

2 medium jalapeño peppers

1 small bunch scallions

Meat

¾ pound sirloin steak (skirt, flank, or strip can be used)

Grocery

1 small bottle ground ginger

Staples

Ground cumin

Dried thyme

Cayenne pepper

Garlic

Olive oil spray

30-minute quick-cooking brown rice

No-sugar-added oil (olive or canola) and vinegar dressing

Salt

Black peppercorns

Jalapeño Rice

½ cup 30-minute quick-cooking brown rice

2 tablespoons no-sugar-added oil (olive or canola) and vinegar dressing

2 medium jalapeno peppers, seeded and chopped (2 tablespoons)

2 scallions, thinly sliced

Salt and freshly ground black pepper

Bring a large saucepan with 2 to 3 quarts water to a boil. Add rice to the saucepan, stir once or twice, and let boil 30 minutes. Alternatively, follow the cooking instructions on the rice package. Reserve 3 tablespoons cooking liquid and place in a serving bowl. Add the dressing to the bowl. Add peppers and scallions. Drain rice and add to bowl. Add salt and pepper to taste. Toss well. Divide and spoon onto 2 steak dinner plates. Make 2 servings.

Per serving: 237 calories, 5.2 grams protein, 34.3 grams carbohydrate, 9.8 grams fat (1.5 saturated), 0 milligram cholesterol, 80 milligrams sodium, 1.5 grams fiber

Chicken and Walnuts in Lettuce Puffs with Sweet and Sour Cabbage and Oranges

Stir fried chicken, walnuts, and vegetables served in lettuce puffs is one of my favorite dishes in a Chinese restaurant. Hoisin sauce spooned over crisp, cool lettuce and then topped with warm chicken and vegetables creates a taste and texture sensation. ● I asked Martin Yan of TV's Yan Can Cook why cooking in a wok at home doesn't produce the same results as when food is prepared in a Chinese restaurant. Here's his advice: Don't overcrowd the wok. Cook small portions. Use a wok that is about 20 inches in diameter; if using a smaller wok, use even smaller portions. Heat the wok until it is almost smoking, then add the oil. Drizzle the oil around the sides, swirling to coat the wok, and wait about 5 seconds before adding the other ingredients.

Chicken and Walnuts in Lettuce Puffs

¼ pound boneless, skinless chicken breasts, cut into ½-inch pieces

1 tablespoon bottled oyster-flavored sauce

2 tablespoons walnut pieces

3 teaspoons sesame oil, divided use

1 teaspoon minced fresh ginger or ½ teaspoon ground ginger

1 medium garlic clove, crushed

¼ cup diced carrots

½ cup diced shiitaki mushrooms

½ cup sliced water chestnuts

½ tablespoon rice vinegar

¼ cup hoisin sauce

8 small iceberg lettuce cups (inner leaves from lettuce that curve into a cup)

Place chicken in a bowl with oyster sauce and let stand 10 minutes. Heat wok over high heat and add walnut pieces. Toast in wok 1 to 2 minutes or until slightly colored. Remove and set aside. Heat wok over high heat. Add 1 teaspoon sesame oil. Add ginger and cook, stirring until fragrant, about 10 seconds. Add chicken and oyster sauce and stir-fry for 1 minute. Add garlic, carrots, mushrooms, and water chestnuts. Stir-fry 2 minutes. Add remaining 2 teaspoons sesame oil and rice vinegar. Cook to heat through a few seconds. Add walnuts and toss to coat. Remove from heat.

To serve: Divide chicken, hoisin sauce, and lettuce cups between 2 dinner plates. Spread a small spoonful of hoisin sauce on a lettuce cup, spoon in some of chicken mixture, wrap in lettuce cup, and eat like a sandwich. Makes 2 servings.

Per serving: 541 calories, 58.3 grams protein, 27.2 grams carbohydrate, 23.6 grams fat (3.6 saturated), 145 milligrams cholesterol, 797 milligrams sodium, 4.1 grams fiber

Helpful Hints

● Use toasted sesame oil if available in your market. It gives a smoky flavor.

● Chinese cabbage is also known as napa cabbage. It has thin, crisp, pale green leaves. Any firm lettuce can be substituted.

● Hoisin sauce is a mixture of soybeans, garlic, chili peppers, and spices. It can be found in the Chinese section of the supermarket.

● Rice vinegar can be bought in the Asian section of the supermarket. One-half tablespoon water mixed with ½ tablespoon distilled white vinegar may be used as a substitute.

Countdown

● Prepare oranges.

● Prepare walnuts and chicken.

● While chicken marinates, prepare all other ingredients.

● Stir-fry Sweet and Sour Cabbage.

● Using same wok, stir-fry the chicken dish.

continues

Chicken and Walnuts in Lettuce Puffs with Sweet and Sour Cabbage and Oranges

continued

Shopping List

Produce

1 small piece fresh ginger or ground ginger

1 small package shiitaki mushrooms (2 ounces needed)

1 small head iceberg lettuce

1 small head Chinese or napa cabbage

1 medium red pepper

2 oranges

Meat

¼ pound boneless, skinless chicken breasts

Grocery

1 small bottle oyster-flavored sauce

1 small bottle sesame oil

1 small bottle hoisin sauce

1 small can sliced water chestnuts

1 small package walnut pieces

Staples

Carrots

Garlic

Rice vinegar

Hot pepper sauce

Sugar substitute

Salt

Sweet and Sour Cabbage

Several drops hot pepper sauce

1 tablespoon hoisin sauce

2 tablespoons Chinese rice vinegar

Sugar substitute equivalent to 2 teaspoons sugar

½ teaspoon salt

1 teaspoon sesame oil

4 cups sliced Chinese or napa cabbage, thinly sliced

1 medium red pepper, seeded and sliced

Mix together hot pepper sauce, hoisin sauce, Chinese rice vinegar, sugar substitute, and salt. Heat wok to smoking and add sesame oil. When oil is smoking, add cabbage and red pepper. Stir-fry 2 minutes. Pour in sauce. Toss well, spoon into a bowl, and let sit until chicken dish is ready. This can be served hot or cold. Do not wash the wok. It can be used for the chicken dish. Makes 2 servings.

Per serving: 81 calories, 2.3 grams protein, 12.8 grams carbohydrate, 3.0 grams fat (0.4 saturated), 0 milligram cholesterol, 691 milligrams sodium, 2.2 grams fiber

Oranges

2 oranges

Peel oranges. Slice in quarters and place on 2 dessert plates. Makes 2 servings.

Per serving: 62 calories, 1.2 grams protein, 15.4 grams carbohydrate, 0.2 gram fat (0 saturated), 0 milligram cholesterol, 0 milligram sodium, 3.1 grams fiber

Steak in Port Wine with French Green Beans and Brown Rice

This typical French bistro dish is a delicious recipe and very simple to prepare. The shallots and mushrooms provide the base for the wine sauce. ● Shallots are in the onion family, but have a milder flavor. They have a teardrop shape and can be found near the onions in the produce department. They are used in many sauces because their cellular structure allows them to melt into the sauce. ● To flambé, if using gas, warm the cognac in the pan for a few seconds and then tip the pan so that the gas flame will ignite the liquid. Remove from the heat and wait for the flame to die down. If using an electric burner, throw a lighted match into the warmed cognac. When the flame dies down, remove the match. For safety, keep a skillet cover nearby to smother flame if necessary. ● Brown rice takes about 45 minutes to cook. There are several brands of quick-cooking brown rice available. Their cooking times range from 10 to 30 minutes. I find the 30-minute rice has more flavor, but any quick-cooking rice will work for this dinner.

Steak in Port Wine

1 teaspoon canola oil

2 (6-ounce) beef tenderloin medallions

Salt and freshly ground black pepper

¼ cup cognac

5 medium shallots, peeled and thinly sliced (1¼ cups)

¼ pound portobello mushrooms, thinly sliced (1½ cups)

¼ cup dry port wine

½ cup fat-free, low-sodium chicken broth

2 tablespoons light cream

2 tablespoons chopped parsley

Heat oil over medium heat in a nonstick skillet just large enough to hold the fillets in one layer. Add the steaks and brown 2 minutes, turn and brown 2 minutes for a 1-inch-thick steak. Add salt and pepper to taste to the cooked side. If steak is 2 to 3 inches thick, lower the heat to medium and sauté the fillets 3 minutes for rare, 5 to 6 minutes for medium-rare. Add the cognac to the steak and flambé. Remove steak to a plate and cover with another plate or aluminum foil to keep warm. Add the shallots to the skillet and sauté until golden, about 2 minutes. Do not let them turn dark brown or black. Add the mushrooms and sauté 3 minutes. Add the port. Raise the heat to high and reduce the sauce for 1 minute. Add the chicken broth and reduce the sauce by half, about 1 minute. Stir in cream, and spoon sauce over steak and rice. Sprinkle with parsley. Makes 2 servings.

Per serving: 470 calories, 38.6 grams protein, 11.7 grams carbohydrate, 19.0 grams fat (7.1 saturated), 115 milligrams cholesterol, 247 milligrams sodium, 0 gram fiber

Helpful Hints

● Beef tenderloin medallions or steaks may not be in the meat case. Ask the butcher to cut two 6-ounce beef fillet medallions for you. Or buy a ¾-pound piece of beef tenderloin and cut it into 2 steaks at home.

● Haricots vert or small French green beans can be found in most supermarkets. They are pencil thin and take only a few minutes to cook. If unavailable, use fresh green beans and cut into 2-inch pieces.

● To save washing another skillet, use same skillet for beans and steak.

● Slice mushrooms and shallots in a food processor fitted with a thin slicing blade.

Countdown

● Start rice.
● Make beans.
● Make steak.

continues

Steak in Port Wine with French Green Beans and Brown Rice continued

French Green Beans

2 teaspoons canola oil
1 medium garlic clove, unpeeled
½ pound haricots vert (French
  green beans), trimmed (2 cups)
Salt and freshly ground
  black pepper

Heat oil in a nonstick skillet on medium-high heat. Add garlic and beans and sauté 5 minutes or until beans are tender but firm. Remove garlic clove and add salt and pepper to taste. Makes 2 servings.

> Per serving: 88 calories, 2.5 grams protein, 10.3 grams carbohydrate, 5.0 gram fat (0.6 saturated), 0 milligram cholesterol, 4 milligrams sodium, 2.2 grams fiber

Brown Rice

⅓ cup 30-minute quick-cooking
  brown rice
Salt and freshly ground black
  pepper to taste

Bring a large saucepan with 2 to 3 quarts of water to a boil. Add the rice and boil 30 minutes or according to package instructions. Drain and add salt and pepper to taste. Divide rice between 2 plates and place steak on top. Spoon sauce over steak and rice. Makes 2 servings.

> Per serving: 85 calories, 2.5 grams protein, 17.5 grams carbohydrate, 0.8 gram fat (0.2 saturated), 0 milligram cholesterol, 0 milligram sodium, 1.0 gram fiber

right carbs
weekend meals

Pan-Seared Tuna with Mango Salsa, Saffron Pilaf, and Lemon Chiffon

Helpful Hints

- *Pan searing requires that the skillet be very hot. Add the fish only when you see smoke rising from the pan.*
- *Use a nonstick skillet that is just large enough to hold the tuna.*
- *Peaches or plums can be substituted for mango.*
- *To cube mango, slice off each side of the mango as close to the seed as possible. Take the mango half in your hand, skin side down. Score the fruit in a crisscross pattern through to the skin. Bend the skin backwards so that the cubes pop up. Slice the cubes away from the skin. Score and slice any fruit left on the pit.*

Countdown

- *Make dessert 2 hours ahead.*
- *Make Saffron Pilaf.*
- *Make salsa.*
- *Make tuna.*

Pan searing is a perfect way to cook fish. The outside becomes crisp while the inside remains tender and moist. Toasting cumin and coriander seeds in the frying pan allows their natural oils to be released for a more concentrated flavor. ● *Brown rice takes about 45 minutes to cook. There are several brands of quick-cooking brown rice available. Their cooking times range from 10 to 30 minutes. The 10-minute rice is needed for this recipe.* ● *The Lemon Chiffon is made with Jell-o gelatin and needs to be made at least 2 hours in advance. For a quick dessert, serve 1 orange per person.*

Pan-Seared Tuna with Mango Salsa

*1 ripe mango, cut into cubes
  (¹⁄₂ pound, about 1 cup)*
2 tablespoons chopped red onion
1 teaspoon ground cumin
1 tablespoon balsamic vinegar
Several drops hot pepper sauce
¹⁄₄ cup chopped fresh cilantro
1 tablespoon cumin seed
1 tablespoon coriander seed
1 teaspoon olive oil
³⁄₄ pound tuna steak
Salt
2 whole wheat rolls

To prepare the salsa, combine mango, red onion, ground cumin, balsamic vinegar, hot pepper sauce, and cilantro in a bowl. Toss well. Taste for seasoning and add more cumin if needed.

To prepare the tuna, place cumin and coriander seeds in a medium nonstick frying pan over medium heat. Toss 2 minutes and remove from heat. Place in a food processor or mini-processor and coarsely chop. Add olive oil and blend a few seconds.

Rinse tuna and pat dry with a paper towel. Spoon the spice mixture over both sides of tuna, pressing the seeds into the fish with the back of the spoon. Heat the same skillet on high. It needs to be smoking before the tuna is added. Brown tuna for 1 minute on one side and turn. Brown 1 minute and lower heat to medium-high. Cook another 3 to 4 minutes. Add a little salt to taste. Remove tuna to 2 plates, spoon salsa on top, and serve with rolls. Makes 2 servings.

Per serving: 322 calories, 37.2 grams protein, 19.6 grams carbohydrate, 10.3 grams fat (2.4 saturated), 59 milligrams cholesterol, 203 milligrams sodium, 1.1 grams fiber

continues

Saffron Pilaf

1 teaspoon olive oil
1 cup 10-minute quick-cooking
brown rice
1 cup water
1/8 teaspoon saffron
Salt and freshly ground
black pepper

Heat olive oil in a medium nonstick skillet over medium heat. Add rice and sauté 1 minute. Add water and saffron. Bring to a simmer and cover. Simmer 15 minutes. Add salt and pepper to taste. Makes 2 servings.

Per serving: 148 calories, 3.8 grams protein, 26.3 grams carbohydrate, 3.5 grams fat (0.5 saturated), 0 milligram cholesterol, 0 milligram sodium, 1.5 grams fiber

Lemon Chiffon

1 package sugar-free lemon Jell-o
gelatin (.32 ounces)
1/2 cup nonfat ricotta cheese

Soften Jell-o gelatin according to package instructions, using 6 large ice cubes instead of cold water for a quick set. Let set in refrigerator 1 hour. Whip with whisk, fold in ricotta cheese. Spoon into 2 glass dessert bowls or dishes and let set 1 hour. Makes 2 servings.

Per serving: 174 calories, 3.6 grams protein, 19.3 grams carbohydrate, 1 gram fat (0.3 saturated), 0 milligram cholesterol, 236 milligrams sodium, 0.6 gram fiber

Shopping List

Produce
1 bunch fresh cilantro
1 ripe mango
1 lime

Dairy
1 small container nonfat
ricotta cheese

Seafood
3/4 pound tuna steak

Grocery
2 whole wheat rolls
1 small bottle cumin seeds
1 small bottle coriander seeds
1 small package saffron
threads
1 package sugar-free, instant
lemon Jell-o

Staples
Red onion
Hot pepper sauce
Balsamic vinegar
Ground cumin
Olive oil
10-minute quick-cooking
brown rice
Salt
Black peppercorns

continues

Helpful Hints

- *Most washed spinach comes in 10-ounce bags. Use half a 10-ounce bag for this recipe.*
- *Fresh cilantro can be used instead of fresh mint. A quick way to chop mint is to snipe the leaves off the stem with a scissors.*

Countdown

- *Marinate chicken.*
- *Start spinach and rice.*
- *Complete chicken.*
- *Complete rice.*

Indian-Spiced Chicken and Rice and Spinach Pilaf

Tandoori chicken with its delicate blend of spices and intriguing aroma is cooked in a clay oven heated by charcoal. A ginger, garlic, coriander, and cayenne yogurt sauce is used as a marinade and sauce for the chicken. For this dinner, I have captured the essence of tandoori chicken with this easy yogurt sauce. Although not made in a special oven, the meal creates the essence of tandoori flavors. ● All of the spices can all be found in the spice section of the supermarket. To help the marinade penetrate the chicken, I make 3 long slits across the chicken. The method of browning the chicken and then covering it to finish cooking keeps the chicken moist and flavorful.

Indian-Spiced Chicken

¾ pound boneless, skinless chicken breasts
1 cup nonfat plain yogurt, drained
¼ cup loosely packed fresh mint leaves plus 2 tablespoons, chopped, divided use
½ inch fresh ginger, peeled and chopped (1 tablespoon)
1 teaspoon ground coriander
Pinch cayenne
Sugar substitute equivalent to 2 teaspoons sugar
2 teaspoons canola oil
1 cup frozen chopped onion
2 medium garlic cloves, crushed
Salt and freshly ground black pepper

Remove fat from chicken and make 3 or 4 long slits in meat to allow marinade to penetrate. Mix yogurt, ¼ cup chopped mint, ginger, coriander, cayenne, and sugar substitute together. Divide in half and reserve half the marinade in a separate bowl. Add chicken to half the marinade and let marinate 10 minutes. Turn once during this time.

Heat oil in a nonstick skillet just large enough to hold chicken in 1 layer over medium-high heat. Remove chicken from marinade and discard marinade. Add onion, garlic, and chicken to the skillet. Brown chicken 3 minutes. Turn and brown 2 minutes. Sprinkle salt and pepper to taste over cooked side. Lower heat to medium. Spoon reserved marinade over chicken, cover, and cook 5 minutes. A meat thermometer should read 160 degrees. Place on 2 dinner plates. Sprinkle with remaining 2 tablespoons chopped mint and serve. Makes 2 servings.

Per serving: 428 calories, 60.8 grams protein, 19.5 grams carbohydrate, 12.6 grams fat (2.5 saturated), 147 milligrams cholesterol, 223 milligrams sodium, 0 gram fiber

continues

Rice and Spinach Pilaf

1 teaspoon canola oil
1 cup frozen chopped onion
5 ounces spinach (about 4 cups)
½ cup basmati rice
1 cup fat-free, low-sodium chicken
    broth
½ teaspoon ground cumin
Salt and freshly ground
    black pepper

Heat oil in a medium-size nonstick skillet on medium-high heat. Add onion and spinach. Sauté 2 minutes. Add rice and sauté 1 minute. Add chicken broth and cumin. When liquid comes to a simmer, lower heat to medium, cover, and simmer 15 minutes. Remove from heat, add salt and pepper to taste and serve. Makes 2 servings.

Per serving: 249 calories, 8.8 grams protein, 47.7 grams carbohydrate, 2.8 grams fat (0.4 saturated), 0 milligram cholesterol, 368 milligrams sodium, 3.6 grams fiber

Shopping List

Produce
1 small piece fresh ginger
1 bag washed, ready-to-eat
    spinach (5 ounces needed)
1 small bunch fresh mint

Dairy
1 small carton nonfat
    plain yogurt

Meat
¾ pound boneless, skinless
    chicken breasts

Grocery
1 small jar ground coriander
1 small package basmati rice

Staples
Garlic
Canola oil
Fat-free, low-sodium chicken
    broth
Sugar substitute
Ground cumin
Frozen chopped onion
Cayenne pepper
Salt
Black peppercorns

Pork Chops with Apple Relish, Toasted Walnut Lentils, and Cranberry Applesauce

Helpful Hints

- *Look for unsweetened applesauce with 100 calories, 30 grams sodium, and 30 grams carbohydrates per cup.*
- *Regular pork chops can be used instead of boneless ones. Either cut meat off the bone before cooking or increase the cooking time for the chops about 5 minutes.*
- *A quick way to chop chives is to snip them with a scissors.*

Countdown

- *Start lentils.*
- *Make pork chops and relish.*
- *Finish lentils.*
- *Make Cranberry Applesauce.*

Sweet and tart apple relish garnishes a sautéed boneless pork chop for this quick weekend dinner. This recipe calls for a Gala apple. It's a sweet, moderately crisp, juicy apple that holds its shape well and adds just the right amount of sweetness to the relish. If you can't find Gala apples, use another type of your choice. ● *You can buy boneless, butterflied pork chops in the supermarket. They have very little fat and cook quickly.* ● *Shallots are in the onion family, but have a milder flavor. They have a teardrop shape and can be found near the onions in the produce department. They are used in many sauces because their cellular structure allows them to melt into the sauce.*

Pork Chops with Apple Relish

1 teaspoon canola oil

2 (6-ounce) boneless loin pork chops

Salt and freshly ground black pepper

1 medium Gala apple, cored and coarsely chopped

1 medium shallot, chopped (about 2 tablespoons)

2 tablespoons apple cider vinegar

Sugar substitute equivalent to 2 teaspoons sugar

Heat canola oil in a small nonstick skillet over medium-high heat. Add pork chops and brown 2 minutes. Turn and brown second side 2 minutes. Add salt and pepper to taste to the cooked side. Reduce heat to medium and cook 4 minutes. A meat thermometer should read 160 degrees.

While pork chops cook, mix apple, shallot, apple cider vinegar, and sugar substitute together in a small bowl. Add salt and pepper to taste.

Place pork chops on 2 individual dinner plates and spoon apple relish on top. Makes 2 servings.

Per serving: 325 calories, 45.5 grams protein, 12.7 grams carbohydrate, 10.1 grams fat (3.0 saturated), 146 milligrams cholesterol, 106 milligrams sodium, 1.9 grams fiber

continues

Toasted Walnut Lentils

1 cup fat-free, low-sodium chicken broth

1 cup water

½ cup dried lentils

2 tablespoons broken walnuts

Salt and freshly ground black pepper

¼ cup snipped chives

Bring chicken broth and water to a rolling boil in a medium-size saucepan over high heat. Slowly add lentils so that the water continues to boil. Reduce the heat to medium-low, cover with a lid, and simmer 20 minutes. Meanwhile place walnuts on a foil-lined baking sheet and toast in a toaster oven or under a broiler for several minutes. Watch them carefully. They burn easily. Remove lid and continue to cook lentils over high heat, until any remaining liquid has been absorbed. Season with salt and pepper to taste. Toss with walnuts and chives. Makes 2 servings.

Per serving: 245 calories, 16.8 grams protein, 29.7 grams carbohydrate, 7.9 grams fat (0.7 saturated), 0 milligram cholesterol, 285 milligrams sodium, 15.4 grams fiber

Cranberry Applesauce

2 cups unsweetened applesauce

2 tablespoons dried cranberries

¼ cup water

Divide applesauce between 2 dessert bowls. Microwave cranberries with water for 1 minute. Drain cranberries, divide in half, and stir into the applesauce. Makes 2 servings.

Per serving: 145 calories, 0.4 gram protein, 42.1 grams carbohydrate, 0.2 gram fat (0.1 saturated), 0 milligram cholesterol, 31 milligrams sodium, 4 grams fiber

entertaining

This section is geared to making parties that don't take all day to prepare. I love to have friends over, but find it hard to spend days shopping and cooking. I also want to serve food that's fun to eat and won't break the calorie bank. These parties let you splurge a little and still keep within the overall guidelines of the low-carbohydrate lifestyle.

They are designed for eight people to show you dishes you can make to follow a theme and create an atmosphere. The foods and quantities fit within the guidelines for the phase indicated at the top of each menu. You may want to make more and have some leftovers rather than run short (some guests may take more of a food they prefer and less of another).

Every detail of these parties has been planned for you including

- A shopping list with the amounts you will need
- A countdown for the days prior to and the day including the party
- The countdown indicates when to buy the ingredients, when to prepare each dish, and how to store and rewarm or prepare them for serving.

Most of the recipes need very little preparation and many can be made ahead. There's almost no last-minute preparation.

Choose from the different party styles to best suit your occasion

- The Buffet for Friends is perfect for football or other sports-related parties, tailgating, picnics, or those times when you have a group over for a Sunday brunch after a family event.
- Prepare the Italian Supper for Friends for simple gatherings or casual Saturday nights. It is perfect for any season of the year.
- The Barbecue dinner is easy to assemble, can be set up outside or in, and creates a fun atmosphere for your entertaining.
- It seems that a majority of guests want to hang out in the kitchen. So, serve the Casual Soup Supper right in the kitchen with the soup in a large pot on the stove and the sandwiches and salad on the kitchen counters.

For the times you want an elegant dinner, the Dinner Party for Eight is your answer. Much of it can be made ahead and there are exact directions for preparing the dishes so that you don't have to spend the evening in the kitchen.

Here are some general guidelines for drinks that will fit any of these parties:

- To keep within the low-carbohydrate guidelines, count on 1 glass of alcohol or wine per person and choose from this list for some other interesting drinks for them to try.
- Make a pitcher of strong-flavored coffee, such as hazelnut or amaretto, and refrigerate. Serve over ice in tall attractive glasses. Be sure to place ice in the pitcher just before serving or serve the ice in a bucket on the side.
- Stay away from flavored syrups for coffee. They usually are made with a sugar syrup base.
- Make a pitcher of flavored iced tea such as peach, berry, or apple cinnamon. Or make a mixture of peach and apple cinnamon tea together. Set out glasses with a slice of the particular type of fruit in each glass.
- Serve no-sugar-added, flavored sparkling water with a twist of lemon or lime.
- Display an assortment of unusual-flavored diet sodas.

Decorate your table for the occasion. Let your table set the atmosphere and create a warm, welcoming feeling. In an interview I had with Susie Coelho, lifestyle expert for the *Today Show* and author of *Susie Coelho's Everyday Styling*, she gave me some tips on how to make your buffet table look rich and attractive.

Decorate around the theme of the meal by using

- Italian pottery and colors for an Italian meal
- The colors of the football teams playing for a Super Bowl or sports party
- Colors from your garden flowers for an outdoor or barbecue party
- A tone-on-tone theme (for example, different shades of white and cream) for an elegant party.

Fill the buffet table with enticing objects. Take your colored napkins and go around the house looking for objects that go with them. Gather them together and see what looks best on the table. These can be pottery, vases, candlesticks, garden baskets, flowerpots, an old child's toy, or miniature wooden wheelbarrow. Select pieces that go with your theme or colors and set them on the table. Remove those that don't look right until you have an attractive display. Use these objects as bases for flower arrangements, napkin and cutlery holders, or just as a design element on the table. This will make your table fun and inviting without having to spend hours preparing a groaning display of food.

entertaining
italian supper
for friends

Italian Supper for Friends

This party fits the guidelines for the Which Carbs section. ● *This Italian meal is perfect for a casual buffet. Most of the recipes can be made ahead, leaving just a few things to do on party day.*

Menu

- *Garden Crudités and Dip*
- *Pollo Tonnato (Italian Chicken with Tuna Sauce)*
- *Lentil and Rice Salad*
- *String Beans with Crumbled Gorgonzola*
- *White Chocolate Whip*

Countdown

Two days before
- *Shop for ingredients.*

One day before
- *Poach chicken and make sauce.*
- *Cut yellow squash for crudités, and store in plastic bags in the refrigerator.*
- *Make Lentil and Rice Salad and place in attractive bowl. Wrap and refrigerate.*
- *Blanch green beans, place in plastic bag, and refrigerate.*

Morning of party
- *Make White Chocolate Whip, place in dessert glasses or dishes, and refrigerate.*
- *Slice fennel, arrange crudités platter, wrap, and refrigerate. Make dip.*
- *Arrange string beans on a platter, wrap, and refrigerate.*
- *Arrange chicken on platter with sauce, pimiento, capers, and olives. Wrap and refrigerate.*

One hour before guests arrive
- *Remove finished dishes from refrigerator to bring to room temperature.*
- *Drizzle dressing on green beans and sprinkle cheese on top.*

Shopping List

(Buy 2 days ahead of party)

Produce
½ pound broccoli florets

1 ½ pounds haricots vert

1 small yellow squash

2 medium fennel bulbs

1 lemon

Shopping List continued

Dairy

1 large carton nonfat plain yogurt (10 ounces needed)

1 carton nonfat ricotta cheese (30 ounces needed)

1 container crumbled Gorgonzola

Meat

8 (6-ounce) boneless, skinless chicken breasts

Grocery

1 small jar honey

1 small package dried lentils

1 small package basmati rice

1 small container saffron threads

1 package pine nuts

1 small jar ground coriander

1 small bottle dry white wine

1 small tin anchovy fillets

1 can sliced sweet pimientos

1 jar capers

1 container pitted black olives (18 needed)

2 packages instant fat-free, sugar-free, white chocolate pudding mix

1 small package semisweet chocolate

Staples

Olive oil spray

Red onions

Garlic

Dijon mustard

Fat-free, low-sodium chicken broth

Reduced-fat mayonnaise

No-sugar-added oil (olive or canola) and vinegar dressing

Olive oil

White tuna packed in water

Lemons

Salt

Black peppercorns

Garden Crudités and Dip

½ pound broccoli florets,
   washed—cut in half, if large

1 small yellow squash, washed and
   sliced diagonally in ¼-inch slices

3 cups sliced fennel (2 medium
   bulbs)

½ cup nonfat plain yogurt

2 tablespoons honey

2 tablespoons Dijon mustard

Arrange the vegetables on a platter or plate. Mix yogurt, honey, and mustard together and place in a small bowl. Or slice the top off a small red cabbage and hollow out the inside. Spoon the dressing into the cabbage and serve near the crudités. Makes 8 servings.

Per serving: 56 calories, 2.2 grams protein, 9.1 grams carbohydrate, 0.4 gram fat (0 saturated), 0 milligram cholesterol, 110 milligrams sodium, 0.8 gram fiber

Helpful Hints

● *Any type of precut vegetables can be added.*

● *Use cut vegetables from the salad bar. Pick and choose the vegetables that are in season.*

● *To slice fennel, cut off stem and leaves and slice the bulb only.*

Lentil and Rice Salad

2 cups fat-free, low-sodium chicken broth

2 cups water, divided use

1 cups lentils, rinsed to remove stones

⅔ cups basmati rice, rinsed

¼ teaspoon saffron threads

Salt and freshly ground black pepper

½ cup pine nuts

2 tablespoons plus 2 teaspoons olive oil, divided use

1½ cups sliced red onion

6 garlic cloves, crushed

¾ teaspoon ground coriander

Bring chicken broth and 1 cup water to a boil in a nonstick skillet on medium-high heat. Add the lentils slowly so that the broth continues to boil. Lower heat to medium. Cover with a lid and simmer 5 minutes. Add rice, saffron, and remaining 1 cup water to the lentils. Bring back to a simmer, cover, and simmer 15 minutes. The liquid will be absorbed and the lentils will be cooked through, but firm. Add salt and pepper to taste.

While lentils and rice cook, heat a nonstick skillet on medium-high heat and add pine nuts. Sauté pine nuts 1 to 2 minutes or until golden. Be careful because the nuts burn easily. Remove and set aside. Heat 2 teaspoons olive oil in the same skillet and add the onion. Sauté, without browning, 5 minutes. Add the garlic and continue to sauté 5 minutes.

Place lentils, rice, and onion in a large bowl and add the remaining 2 tablespoons oil, coriander, and salt and pepper to taste. Toss well. Taste for seasoning and add more salt and pepper, if needed. Sprinkle toasted pine nuts on top and serve. Makes 8 servings.

Per serving: 231 calories, 9.2 grams protein, 29.6 grams carbohydrate, 5.1 grams fat (0.7 saturated), 0 milligram cholesterol, 144 milligrams sodium, 7.3 grams fiber

String Beans with Crumbled Gorgonzola

1 1/2 pounds haricots vert (small
    green beans)
3 tablespoons no-sugar-added oil
    (olive or canola) and vinegar
    dressing
Salt and freshly ground black
    pepper
4 ounces crumbled Gorgonzola

Bring a medium-size pot of water to a boil. Trim beans and add to boiling water. As soon as the water comes back to a boil, drain and plunge beans into a bowl of ice water. Drain. Place on platter, drizzle dressing over the top and toss. Add salt and pepper to taste. Sprinkle cheese on top. Makes 8 servings.

Per serving: 64 calories, 3.5 grams protein,
5.1 grams carbohydrate, 3.6 grams fat (2.1 saturated),
10 milligrams cholesterol, 194 milligrams sodium,
1.1 grams fiber

Helpful Hints

● A quick way to trim beans is to line them up with the ends together and slice off the tips. Turn bunch around to opposite ends, line them up, and slice off the tips.

● Large green beans can be used. Cut them into 4-inch lengths before blanching.

● Any type of blue-veined cheese can be used.

Helpful Hint

- *The chicken can be poached and the sauce can be made the day before and refrigerated.*
- *Save and freeze the remaining poaching liquid. It makes a wonderful broth for other recipes.*

Pollo Tonnato (Chicken in Tuna Sauce)

This is a traditional summer Italian dish that is perfect for buffets. The secret to keeping the chicken moist is to gently poach it and let it cool in the poaching liquid.

8 (6-ounce) boneless, skinless chicken breasts
½ cup dry white wine
1 cup fat-free, low-sodium chicken broth
Salt and freshly ground black pepper
6 anchovy fillets
1½ cups (9 ounces) solid white tuna packed in water
⅔ cup reduced-fat mayonnaise
⅔ cup nonfat plain yogurt
1½ teaspoon lemon juice
2 large pimientos, thinly sliced
6 tablespoons capers, drained and rinsed
18 pitted black olives, cut in half

Remove fat from chicken. Add wine and chicken broth to a large saucepan. Bring to a boil on medium-high heat. Add chicken and then enough warm water to make sure all of the chicken is covered by liquid. Bring to a simmer, lower heat to medium-low and gently simmer, uncovered, 5 minutes. Do not boil the chicken. Remove from heat and let chicken cool in the liquid 15 minutes (reserve ½ cup poaching liquid). Sprinkle chicken with salt and pepper to taste.

While chicken cools, make the sauce. Rinse anchovy fillets and place in the bowl of a food processor with tuna, mayonnaise, and yogurt. Process until smooth. Add poaching liquid and continue to process. Add lemon juice and process to blend into sauce.

To serve, remove chicken from liquid and place on serving platter. Spoon enough sauce over chicken to coat. Serve remaining sauce on the side. Lay pimiento strips across chicken. Sprinkle capers over chicken and arrange the olives attractively. Cover and refrigerate until needed. Bring to room temperature before serving.

Per serving: 412 calories, 59.9 grams protein, 6.8 grams carbohydrate, 17.2 grams fat (3.4 saturated), 153 milligrams cholesterol, 1057 milligrams sodium, 0.7 gram fiber

tuna with mango   p162

White Chocolate Whip

3 ¾ cups nonfat ricotta cheese

2 cups water

½ cup fat-free, sugar-free instant
white chocolate pudding mix

4 teaspoons grated semisweet
chocolate

Whisk ricotta cheese and water together until smooth. This can be done in a food processor. Add the white chocolate pudding powder and whisk until smooth. Divide between 8 dessert bowls. Sprinkle ½ teaspoon grated chocolate on top of each dish. Refrigerate. Makes 8 servings.

Per serving: 114 calories, 0.1 gram protein,
4.9 grams carbohydrate, 0.2 gram fat (0.1 saturated),
0 milligram cholesterol, 272 milligrams sodium,
0 gram fiber

Helpful Hint

● Any flavor fat-free, sugar-tree instant pudding mix can be used.

entertaining
dinner party
for eight

Dinner Party for Eight

This dinner party fits the nutritional guidelines for the Which Carbs phase. ● No need to spend all day making an elegant dinner party. These recipes are easy to make and you and your guests can enjoy the evening without worrying about the calories and carbs.

Menu

- *Bruschetta*
- *Game Hens in Red Wine*
- *Wild and Brown Rice with Toasted Pecans*
- *Asparagus with Red Pepper*
- *Radicchio, Endive, and Watercress Salad*
- *Berry Cups with Almond Sauce*

Countdown

Two days ahead
- *Shop for ingredients.*

One day ahead
- *Make Game Hens in Red Wine. Place in ovenproof casserole or dish, with their sauce. Cover and refrigerate.*
- *Make Wild and Brown Rice. Place in an oven-to-table dish, cover, and refrigerate.*
- *Make Almond Sauce for dessert. Cover and refrigerate.*

Morning of the party
- *Assemble berry cups without sauce and wrap and refrigerate.*
- *Prepare asparagus ready for the oven. Cut off the woody ends, place on baking sheets, roll in olive oil, and place in refrigerator.*
- *Wash watercress, radicchio, and endive; spin dry and place in salad bowl. Cover with plastic wrap and refrigerate.*
- *Make bruschetta topping and refrigerate.*

One hour before guests arrive
- *Remove game hens, rice, asparagus, berries, and sauce from refrigerator.*

Thirty minutes before guests arrive
- *Preheat oven to 300 degrees.*
- *Place hens in their sauce and rice in oven for 30 minutes to warm through.*
- *Remove salad from refrigerator and toss with dressing.*
- *Spoon topping for bruschetta on toasts and arrange on serving tray.*

Before dessert
- *Spoon sauce over berries just before serving.*

Shopping List (Buy 2 days ahead of party except seafood)

Produce

1 medium tomato

1 medium head radicchio

10 ounces Belgian endive

1 bunch watercress

2 pounds asparagus

¾ pound button mushrooms

1 package broccoli florets (10 ounces needed)

Mixture of raspberries, strawberries and blueberries (2½ pounds berries needed)

Dairy

1 carton reduced-fat sour cream (12 ounces needed)

Meat

4 Cornish game hens, about 2 pounds each

Grocery

1 jar/can sweet pimientos (16 ounces needed)

1 package Italian or French rusks, 3 inches diameter

1 package slivered almonds

1 package pine nuts

1 bottle almond extract

1 bottle red wine (Beaujolais or Burgundy)

Staples

30-minute quick-cooking brown rice

Olive oil spray

Red onion

Yellow onion

Carrots

Garlic

Fat-free, low-sodium chicken broth

Olive oil

Balsamic vinegar

No-sugar-added oil (olive or canola) and vinegar dressing

Sugar substitute

Salt

Black peppercorns

Bruschetta

Olive oil spray
1 cup sliced red onion
2 garlic cloves
1 cup diced tomatoes
½ tablespoon olive oil
1 teaspoon balsamic vinegar
Salt and freshly ground
    black pepper
8 Italian or French rusks, 3 inches
    in diameter

Heat a nonstick skillet on medium-high heat. Spray with olive oil spray and add onion and garlic. Sauté 10 minutes. The onion should be golden. Remove from heat and toss with tomatoes. Add olive oil, balsamic vinegar, and salt and pepper to taste. Place in a bowl and refrigerate until needed.

To serve, spoon tomato mixture onto toast and place on serving platter.

Per serving: 56 calories, 1.6 grams protein, 7.9 grams carbohydrate, 1.9 grams fat (0.4 saturated), 0 milligram cholesterol, 39 milligrams sodium, 0.5 gram fiber

Helpful Hint

- Whole wheat toast can be substituted for the rusks.

Radicchio, Endive, and Watercress Salad

Helpful Hint

- *Belgian endive should not be placed in water to clean. The leaves will turn brown. Just remove any damaged outer leaves and then wipe with a damp paper towel.*

1 medium head radicchio

2 cups watercress

2 medium heads Belgian endive (4 cups sliced)

5 tablespoons no-sugar-added oil (olive or canola) and vinegar dressing

Wash radicchio and watercress and spin dry. Cut about 1 inch off flat end of endive and remove any torn or brown outer leaves. Wipe endive with a damp paper towel. Tear radicchio leaves into bite-size pieces. Break large stems off watercress. Slice endive into 1-inch circles. When salad is dry, place in a salad bowl, cover with plastic wrap, and refrigerate. Just before serving, toss with the dressing.

Per serving: 56 calories, 0.7 gram protein, 1.9 grams carbohydrate, 5.4 grams fat (1.9 saturated), 0 milligram cholesterol, 59 milligrams sodium, 0.2 gram fiber

Game Hens in Red Wine

4 Cornish game hens, about
   2 pounds each

Olive oil spray

2 cups sliced yellow onion

2 medium carrots, sliced (1 cup)

4 medium garlic cloves, crushed

1⅓ cups red wine (Beaujolais or
   Burgundy)

1⅓ cups fat-free, low-sodium
   chicken broth

4 cups sliced button mushrooms

Salt and freshly ground black
   pepper

Remove the fat from the cavity of hens and split the hens in half. Heat 2 large nonstick skillets just large enough to hold the hen halves in 1 layer over medium-high heat. Spray with olive oil spray. Brown the hens on both sides, about 5 minutes. Remove to a plate and pour off any excess fat. Add the onion, carrots, and garlic to the skillet. Sauté until the vegetables start to shrivel, about 5 minutes. Return hen halves to the pan, lower the heat to medium, and cover with a lid. Let cook until the halves are cooked through, about 20 minutes. A meat thermometer should read 170 degrees for white meat and 180 degrees for dark meat. Remove hens to a dish and cover with aluminum foil to keep warm. Pour off any remaining fat, add wine, and scrape the brown bits from the bottom of the skillet while the wine simmers for about 2 minutes. Add the chicken broth and mushrooms. Simmer 2 more minutes. Remove skin from hens and add salt and pepper to taste. If serving immediately, return the hens to the pan and warm through. If serving later, place the hens on an ovenproof serving platter and spoon sauce and vegetables on top. Cover and refrigerate. An hour before serving, remove from refrigerator and let stand at room temperature about 30 minutes. Place, covered with foil or a lid, in a 300 degree oven for 20 to 30 minutes or until warmed through. Makes 8 servings.

Per serving: 260 calories, 35.2 grams protein, 7.0 grams carbohydrate, 6.3 grams fat (1.6 saturated), 153 milligrams cholesterol, 215 milligrams sodium, 0.2 gram fiber

Helpful Hints

- Ask butcher to cut game hens in half.
- You will need two 12-inch nonstick skillets to hold the hens in 1 layer. Or cook them in 2 batches.
- Slice vegetables in a food processor fitted with a slicing blade.

Brown Rice with Toasted Pine Nuts

1 cup 30-minute quick-cooking
    brown rice
4 cups broccoli florets
3 tablespoons pine nuts
1 tablespoon olive oil
Salt and freshly ground
    black pepper

Fill a large saucepan with 2 to 3 quarts cold water. Add rice, cover with a lid, and bring to a boil over high heat. When water comes to a boil, remove the lid, lower heat to medium-low and boil for 25 minutes. Add broccoli and continue to boil 5 minutes. While rice boils, place pine nuts on a foil-lined tray and toast in a toaster oven or under a broiler 2 to 3 minutes or until golden. Be careful because the pine nuts burn easily.

When rice is cooked through, drain and toss with oil and salt and pepper to taste. Place in a serving bowl and sprinkle pine nuts on top.

Recipe may be made ahead until this point. Place rice in oven-to-tableware dish and store in the refrigerator. Before serving, bring to room temperature and place in preheated oven with chicken for 30 minutes. Remove from oven and serve. Makes 8 servings.

Per serving: 104 calories, 3.2 grams protein, 15.5 grams carbohydrate, 2.6 grams fat (0.4 saturated), 0 milligram cholesterol, 10 milligrams sodium, 1.4 grams fiber

Roasted Asparagus with Pimientos

½ tablespoon olive oil

Salt and freshly ground
black pepper

2 pounds asparagus, ends trimmed

2 cups pimientos, cut in ½-inch
pieces

Preheat oven to 400 degrees. Line a baking tray with aluminum foil and spoon oil onto foil. Add salt and pepper to taste. Add asparagus and roll in oil, making sure all spears are coated with oil and salt and pepper. Spread asparagus out to form 1 layer and roast in oven 5 minutes. Remove asparagus and turn. Roast 10 more minutes for thick spears, 5 more minutes for thin ones. Remove from oven and arrange spears in straight rows on an oval serving platter. Sprinkle pimientos over top. Makes 8 servings.

Per serving: 33 calories, 2.0 grams protein, 5.0 grams carbohydrate, 1.1 grams fat (0.2 saturated), 0 milligram cholesterol, 8 milligrams sodium, 2.4 grams fiber

Helpful Hint

● Asparagus takes only 10 minutes in oven. Roasting intensifies flavor. Place in oven just before serving.

Berry Cups with Almond Sauce

8 cups berries (mixture of
   raspberries, blueberries, and
   strawberries)
2 teaspoons almond extract
Sugar substitute equivalent to
   2 teaspoons sugar
1 cup reduced-fat sour cream
3 tablespoons slivered almonds

Place berries in 8 small ramekins. Mix almond extract and sugar substitute into sour cream and spoon or dollop sauce on top of each one. Toast almonds in a toaster oven for 1 minute or sauté in a skillet until just turning golden. Be careful toasting the almonds as they burn easily. Sprinkle almonds on top of sauce.
Makes 8 servings.

Per serving: 134 calories, 3 grams protein, 17.3 grams carbohydrate, 6.8 grams fat (2.7 saturated), 15 milligrams cholesterol, 20 milligrams sodium, 6.3 grams fiber

entertaining
casual soup supper

Casual Soup Supper

This meal fits the nutritional guidelines for the Right Carbs phase. ● *Whenever we have friends over, it seems that everyone ends up standing around the kitchen. I planned this party so that the kitchen is part of the fun. I make the soup and leave it in a large, colorful saucepan on the stove with a ladle in the soup. The bowls are nearby and people can help themselves. The sandwiches and salad are placed on the countertop. Everyone can help themselves on their way to finding a seat at the table.*

Menu
● *Creamy Wild Mushroom Soup*
● *Grilled Grouper Sandwich*
● *Three Bean Salad*
● *Mango Fool*

Countdown

Two days ahead
● *Shop for most ingredients except the grouper.*

One day ahead
● *Make soup, cover, and refrigerate.*

Morning of the party
● *Buy grouper.*
● *Make Mango Fool, place in attractive glass, and refrigerate.*
● *Make salad. Place in serving bowl. Cover and refrigerate.*

One hour ahead
● *Prepare ingredients for grouper sandwich.*
● *Remove salad from refrigerator.*
● *Remove soup from refrigerator.*

Fifteen minutes before guests arrive
● *Marinate grouper.*

When guests arrive
● *Place soup on stove and heat. When soup is hot, lower heat to extra low and leave until served.*
● *Make grouper sandwich just before serving.*
● *Remove Mango Fool from refrigerator.*

Shopping List (Buy 2 days ahead of party except seafood)

Produce

1 bunch fresh dill

1 bunch scallions (6 scallions needed)

¾ pound sliced portobello mushrooms

2 medium tomatoes

1 medium Vidalia or other sweet onion

½ pound green beans

½ pound yellow wax beans

2 medium ripe mangoes (1 pound)

1 bunch fresh mint

Dairy

1 small carton heavy cream (4 ounces needed)

4 cartons nonfat, sugar-free mango or tropical fruit yogurt (32 ounces needed)

Grocery

1 small package dried cèpes (mushrooms)

Seafood

8 (6-ounce) grouper fillets (purchase on the day of the party)

Staples

Red kidney beans (18 ounces needed)

Yellow onion

Olive oil spray

Balsamic vinegar

No-sugar-added oil (olive or canola) and vinegar dressing

Flour

Ground nutmeg

Multigrain bread

Fat-free, low-sodium chicken broth

Mayonnaise

Lemons

Salt

Black peppercorns

Creamy Wild Mushroom Soup

Helpful Hints

- *Slice onion and mushrooms in a food processor fitted with a ¼-inch slicing blade.*
- *Cook the onion until it is transparent, but not brown, to give the soup a sweet flavor.*
- *Morel mushrooms can be substituted.*
- *The soup can be made a day in advance. It will thicken on standing. Stir in a little broth when rewarming.*

Many "wild" mushrooms are cultivated and don't have a strong flavor of the woods. Dried cèpes (called porcini in Italy) that have been gathered in the woods add a depth of flavor to this soup. ● The secret to this soup is cooking the onion until it is sweet. Ground nutmeg gives the soup an intriguing flavor.

½ cup dried cèpe mushrooms
5 cups hot water, divided use
Olive oil spray
1 large yellow onion, sliced (2 cups)
¾ pound sliced portobello mushrooms (6 cups)
1 tablespoon flour
4 cups fat-free, low-sodium chicken broth
½ teaspoon ground nutmeg
Salt and freshly ground black pepper
8 tablespoons heavy cream

Add dried cèpes to 1 cup hot water and let stand 5 minutes. Drain, reserving the liquid, and slice. Strain liquid 2 to 3 times to remove sand.

Heat a large saucepan over medium-high heat and spray with olive oil spray. Add the onion and sauté 2 minutes. Reduce heat to medium and continue to cook onion until golden, about 5 minutes. Do not brown onion. Add the portobello mushrooms and sauté 2 minutes, stirring 1 or 2 times. Sprinkle flour on top and stir until absorbed, 1 minute. Add chicken broth and remaining 4 cups water. Lift reconstituted mushrooms from the hot water with a slotted spoon and add to the soup. Place a paper towel in a sieve and strain the mushroom liquid into the soup. Bring to a boil. Simmer 10 minutes. Add nutmeg and salt and pepper to taste.

Remove 1 cup soup to a blender or food processor and purée. Return to the soup. Spoon cream into soup and mix well. Taste for seasoning, adding more if necessary. Makes 8 servings.

Per serving: 102 calories, 2.9 grams protein, 5.4 grams carbohydrate, 7.4 grams fat (3.8 saturated), 21 milligrams cholesterol, 288 milligrams sodium, 0 gram fiber

Grilled Grouper Sandwich

Grilling fish gives great flavor. Grill outside, or for ease, use a stove-top grill or simply sauté fish in skillet. Jacques Pépin once showed me this method for grilling fish in advance. Sear the fish on the grill about 1 hour before needed and then place in a 200 degree oven to finish cooking for about 30 minutes. For a 1-inch-thick fillet, sear 2 minutes per side and then place in oven.

8 (6-ounce) grouper fillets

2 cups balsamic vinegar

1/2 cup mayonnaise

2 tablespoons lemon juice

1 1/2 cups snipped fresh dill, divided use

Salt and freshly ground black pepper

16 slices multigrain bread

8 slices Vidalia or other sweet onion, about 1 cup

8 slices tomato

Heat grill or preheat gas grill. Rinse grouper and pat dry with paper towel. Place in a self-seal plastic bag and add balsamic vinegar. Marinate 15 minutes.

Meanwhile, mix mayonnaise with lemon juice and fold in 1 cup dill, reserving 1/2 cup for garnish. Add salt and pepper to taste.

Remove grouper from bag and pat dry with paper towel. Place on grill 4 inches from heat or on preheated stove-top grill. Grill 2 minutes per side. Salt and pepper cooked side. While grouper grills, toast the bread on the grill, or in a toaster, 1 minute per side.

To serve, spread each slice of toast with a layer of mayonnaise. Place a grouper fillet on each slice. Place onion slices on the grouper and finish with tomato slices. Sprinkle with reserved dill. Serve as open sandwiches.

Makes 8 servings.

Per serving: 455 calories, 36.8 grams protein, 38.9 grams carbohydrate, 14.7 grams fat (2.5 saturated), 62 milligrams cholesterol, 570 milligrams sodium, 1.2 grams fiber

Helpful Hints

- *Ask for the skin to be removed when you buy the fish.*
- *A quick way to chop dill is to snip the leaves with a scissors.*
- *Make sure the grill grates are clean and spray them with vegetable cooking spray before grilling grouper.*
- *Any type of firm, white, non-oily fish fillet can be used.*

Helpful Hint

- *To set the color of the beans, plunge them into ice water after they are blanched. Fill a roasting pan with water and ice cubes and place near the sink. As soon as the beans are drained, plunge them into the ice water. When they are cold, drain.*

Three Bean Salad

3 cups green beans, trimmed and cut into 1-inch pieces (½ pound)

3 cups yellow wax beans, trimmed and cut into 1-inch pieces (½ pound)

2 cups cooked red kidney beans, rinsed and drained

6 scallions, sliced (1 cup)

6 tablespoons no-sugar-added oil (olive or canola) and vinegar dressing

Salt and freshly ground black pepper

Bring a large saucepan filled with water to a boil. Add the green and yellow beans. As soon as the water returns to a boil, drain and refresh under ice cold water. Place in a large serving bowl and add the kidney beans, scallions, and dressing. Toss well. Add salt and pepper to taste. Toss once more. Makes 8 servings.

Per serving: 141 calories, 4.4 grams protein, 17.1 grams carbohydrate, 6.7 grams fat (1.0 saturated), 0 milligram cholesterol, 61 milligrams sodium, 2.2 grams fiber

casual soup supper p188

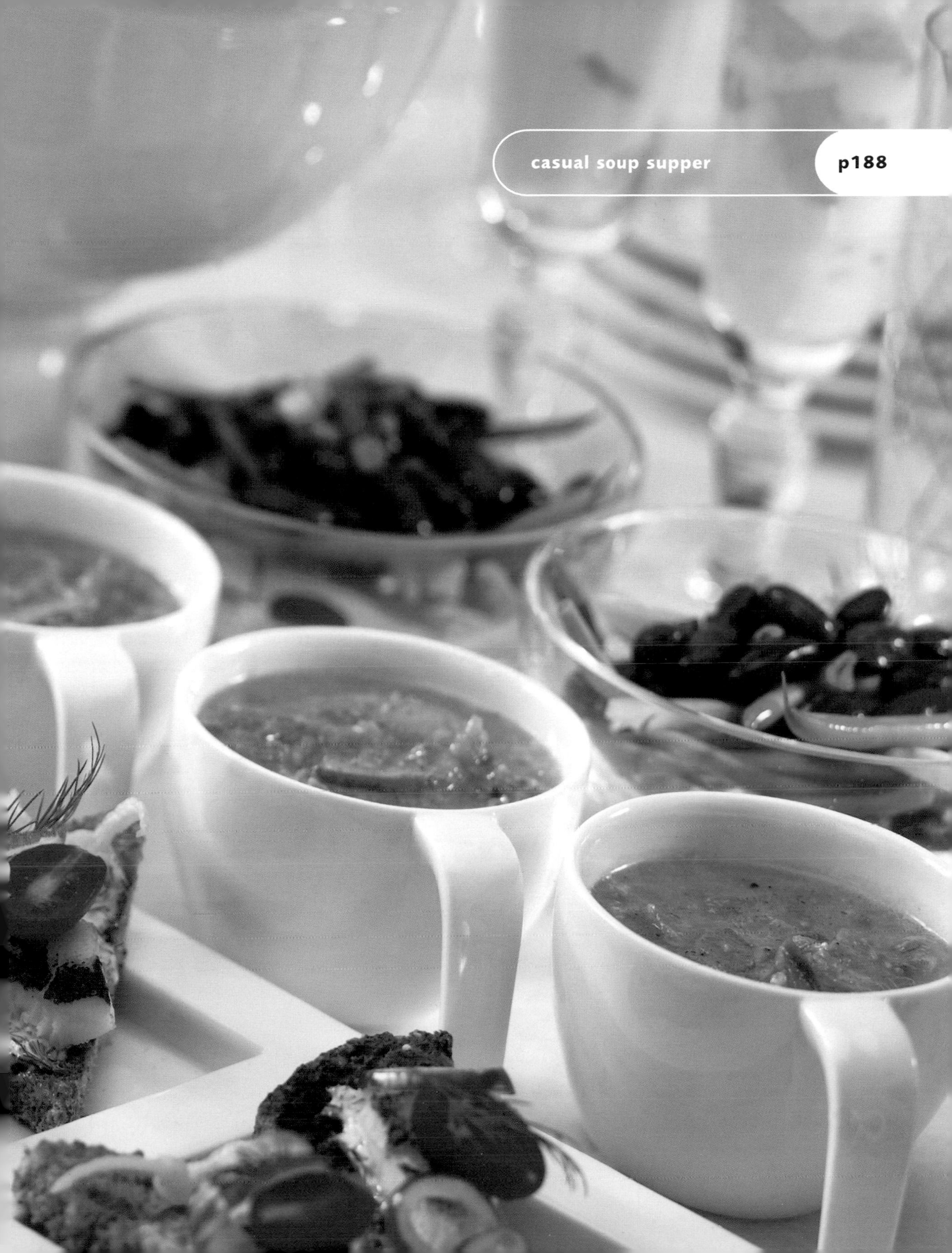

Mango Fool

I was introduced to luscious, creamy fruit fools when I first moved to England. It is a rich pudding, normally made with tart green gooseberries. I have adapted this idea using fresh mangoes and yogurt.

2 ripe mangoes, cubed (1 pound)
4 cups nonfat, sugar-free mango
*   or tropical fruit yogurt*
8 small mint sprigs

Fold the mango cubes into the yogurt and spoon into 8 attractive martini glasses or dessert bowls. Arrange a mint sprig in each glass. Refrigerate until 15 minutes before needed. Let come to room temperature before serving.
Makes 8 servings.

Per serving: 104 calories, 5.8 grams protein, 20.3 grams carbohydrate, 0.2 gram fat (0 saturated), 3 milligrams cholesterol, 96 milligrams sodium, 0.6 gram fiber

Helpful Hint

● *To cube a mango, slice off each side as close to the seed as possible. Cut a 1-inch piece from one half. Remove the skin from the slice and cut into 6 thin strips for a garnish. Take the mango half in your hand, skin side down. Score the fruit in a crisscross pattern through to the skin. Bend the skin backwards so that the cubes pop up. Slice the cubes away from the skin. Repeat with the other half. Score and slice any fruit left on the pit.*

entertaining
buffet for friends

Buffet for Friends

This meal fits the nutritional guidelines for the Right Carbs phase. ● *Super Bowl, tailgate, brunch, or family gatherings all call for grazing foods that, when placed on a table, invite everyone to help themselves. This party needs very little attention during the festivities, leaving you to join in the fun.*

Menu

- *Key Lime-Mustard–Sauced Shrimp*
- *Roasted Meat Platter with Horseradish and Honey Mustard Dressing*
- *Tomato Platter*
- *Pasta Salad*
- *Frozen Yogurt Berry Cup*

Countdown

Two days ahead

- *Shop for ingredients.*

One day ahead

- *Arrange meat platter, wrap, and refrigerate.*
- *Make sauces for meats. Cover and refrigerate.*
- *Make sauce for shrimp.*
- *Poach shrimp. Cover and refrigerate.*

Morning of the party

- *Arrange shrimp on serving platter, wrap, and refrigerate.*
- *Measure frozen yogurt and place in dessert bowls. Place in freezer.*
- *Slice tomatoes and assemble tomato platter.*
- *Make pasta salad.*

One hour before guests arrive

- *Remove shrimp, meat, and sauces from refrigerator and set on buffet table. Place shrimp sauce near shrimp and meat sauces near meat platter. Drizzle tomatoes with Honey Mustard Sauce. Place bread for meat platter in basket.*
- *Remove yogurt bowls from freezer and sprinkle with berries fifteen minutes before serving dessert.*

continues

Buffet for Friends continued

Shopping List (Buy 2 days ahead of party except seafood)

Produce

½ head red leaf lettuce

1 bunch chives

1 bunch watercress

2 large red tomatoes

2 large yellow tomatoes

1 bunch dill

1 package broccoli florets (5 ounces needed)

1 medium cucumber

2 medium red bell peppers

2½ pounds fresh raspberries

Dairy

1 carton nonfat, plain yogurt (10 ounces needed)

Deli

¾ pound sliced lean deli roast beef

¾ pound sliced roast turkey breast

¾ pound lean sliced ham (no honey-baked or glazed)

Seafood

1½ pounds shrimp, peeled and deveined

Grocery

1 bottle key lime juice

1 bottle horseradish

1 jar honey mustard

½ pound whole wheat penne or other whole wheat short cut pasta

1 container low-fat, frozen strawberry yogurt (32 ounces needed)

2 packages thin sliced rye bread (32 slices needed)

Staples

Lemons

Mayonnaise

Dijon mustard

Reduced-fat mayonnaise

Salt

Black peppercorns

Key Lime-Mustard–Sauced Shrimp

1½ pounds shrimp, peeled and deveined

6 tablespoons mayonnaise

2 teaspoons Dijon mustard

1½ tablespoons key lime juice

Arrange shrimp in a circle, tails pointed out, on a serving platter. Mix mayonnaise, mustard, and key lime juice together in a small bowl. Place the bowl in the center of the platter.

Makes 8 servings.

Per serving: 167 calories, 17.4 grams protein, 1.1 grams carbohydrate, 9.8 grams fat (1.4 saturated), 134 milligrams cholesterol, 216 milligrams sodium, 0 gram fiber

Helpful Hints

- Shelled shrimp is available at most supermarket seafood counters. The slightly higher cost is worth the time saved.
- If you're pressed for time, buy shrimp already cooked from the seafood department of the supermarket.
- You can substitute lemon or lime juice for key lime juice

Roasted Meat Platter with Horseradish Sauce and Honey Mustard Sauce

½ head red leaf lettuce

¾ pound sliced lean deli roast beef

¾ pound sliced roast turkey breast

¾ pound lean sliced ham
   (no honey-baked or glazed)

¼ cup reduced-fat mayonnaise

1 ¼ cups light plain yogurt,
   divided use

1 ½ tablespoons horseradish

¼ cup snipped chives

1 ½ tablespoons honey mustard

32 slices thin-sliced rye bread
   (or 16 slices regular-sliced
   rye bread)

To prepare the meat platter, line a serving platter with lettuce leaves. Place meat in radiating rows from the center of the platter to the edge, folding the slices in half and overlapping them. The folded edge should show.

To prepare the horseradish sauce, mix the mayonnaise, ½ cup yogurt, horseradish, and chives together and place in a small bowl. Serve with meat platter.

To prepare the Honey Mustard Sauce, mix the remaining ¾ cup yogurt and honey mustard together and place in a small bowl. Serve with the meat platter.

Place bread in a basket near the meat for people to make their own sandwiches.
Makes 8 servings.

Per serving: 453 calories, 39.1 grams protein, 43.8 grams carbohydrate, 12.3 grams fat (2.9 saturated), 87 milligrams cholesterol, 1091 milligrams sodium, 2.1 grams fiber

Tomato Platter

1 to 2 tablespoons Honey Mustard
Sauce from the Roasted Meat
Platter
2 large red tomatoes
2 large yellow tomatoes
1 bunch watercress, for garnish

Slice tomatoes and alternate red and yellow slices on a serving platter. Drizzle 1 to 2 tablespoons Honey Mustard Sauce on top. Place sprigs of watercress on the side for a garnish. Makes 8 servings.

Per serving: 46 calories, 2.4 grams protein, 7.6 grams carbohydrate, 0.4 gram fat (0 saturated), 1.0 milligram cholesterol, 29 milligrams sodium, 0 gram fiber

Pasta Salad

¼ cup reduced-fat mayonnaise

2 tablespoons freshly squeezed lemon juice

¼ cup snipped fresh dill

1³/₄ cups uncooked whole wheat penne or other whole wheat short pasta (½ pound)

2 cups small broccoli florets

1 cup peeled, seeded, and cubed cucumber

2 cups cubed red bell pepper

Salt and freshly ground black pepper to taste.

Place a large saucepan with 2 to 3 quarts water over high heat to boil. Mix mayonnaise, lemon juice and dill together in a large serving bowl. Add pasta to boiling water and cook 5 minutes. Add broccoli and continue to cook 4 minutes or until pasta is cooked but still firm. Drain and add to serving bowl. Add cucumber, red pepper, and salt and pepper to taste. Makes 8 servings.

Per serving: 123 calories, 4.7 grams protein, 21.4 grams carbohydrate, 3.0 grams fat (0.6 saturated), 3 milligrams cholesterol, 66 milligrams sodium, 3.3 grams fiber

Frozen Yogurt Berry Cup

*4 cups low-fat, frozen strawberry
  yogurt*
4 cups fresh raspberries

Spoon yogurt into 8 dessert bowls and sprinkle berries on top. Makes 8 servings.

Per serving: 151 calories, 3.6 grams protein,
27.1 grams carbohydrate, 3.4 grams fat
(1.5 saturated), 10 milligrams cholesterol,
80 milligrams sodium, 2.9 grams fiber

Helpful Hints

- *Any fresh berries can be used.*
- *The frozen yogurt can be spooned into dessert bowls and placed in the freezer in the morning. They only need to be removed and sprinkled with berries just before serving. They will also hold for about $1/2$ hour out of the freezer this way.*

entertaining
barbecue party

Barbecue Party

The meal fits the nutritional guidelines for the Right Carbs phase. ● *"Let's have a barbecue"
is an invitation that brings smiles to everyone. Grilling is popular year-round and the idea of
cooking outside brings sunny thoughts to most of us, even in the winter months.* ● *Most
barbecued foods are coated with sugary sauces that have a lot of carbs. This simple barbecue
party captures the flavors of the grill without the carbohydrates.* ● *It's easiest to serve this
meal buffet-style.*

Menu

● *Spicy Tuna Spread*
● *No-Fuss Salad Bar*
● *Lime Barbecued Chicken with Black Bean Sauce*
● *Green Bean and Orzo Salad*
● *Melon with Marinated Strawberries and Hot Cookies*

Countdown

Two days ahead

● *Shop for ingredients.*

One day ahead

● *Make Spicy Tuna Spread.*
● *Make black bean sauce for chicken. Cover and refrigerate.*
● *Prepare and blanch onion and red pepper for chicken recipe. Cover and refrigerate.*
● *Make strawberry sauce and place in a bowl. Cover and refrigerate.*

Morning of the party

● *Place ingredients for salad bar in attractive bowls. Cover and refrigerate.*
● *Make Green Bean and Orzo Salad. Cover and refrigerate.*
● *Cut melon into slices and place in bowl. Cover and refrigerate.*
● *Cut cucumber slices for tuna spread. Wrap and refrigerate.*

One hour before guests arrive

● *Marinate chicken, covered, in refrigerator.*
● *Preheat grill, if using charcoal.*
● *Remove tuna spread, black bean sauce, red pepper and onion, green bean and orzo
salad, and strawberry sauce from the refrigerator.*
● *Arrange melon on individual dessert plates. Cover with plastic wrap and set aside.*
● *Set up salad bar on buffet table.*
● *If you prefer not to bake the cookies last minute, preheat oven for cookies and bake
them about 1 hour before guests arrive.*

continues

Countdown continued

Fifteen minutes before guests arrive

- *Place black bean sauce in a saucepan over low heat to heat through.*
- *Spread tuna on cucumber slices and place on serving platter.*
- *Preheat gas grill.*
- *While guests are having drinks and hors d'oeuvres, grill chicken and place on platter in 200 degree oven to keep warm.*

To serve meal

- *Spoon half the black bean sauce onto serving platter, place chicken on top and sprinkle with blanched onion and red pepper. Serve the remaining sauce in a bowl next to the chicken platter. Place on buffet table.*
- *Place green bean and orzo salad on buffet table.*

To serve dessert

- *Preheat oven and place cookies in oven while entrée dishes are being cleared.*
- *Spoon strawberry sauce over melon and place cookie on side.*

Shopping List (Buy 2 days ahead of party except seafood)

Produce

1 bunch basil leaves

1 small bunch parsley

1 small bunch cilantro

2 medium cucumbers

2 bags washed, ready-to-eat lettuce

1 bag shredded, washed, ready-to-eat carrots

2 bags shredded, washed, ready-to-eat red cabbage (4 cups needed)

2 bags washed, ready-to-eat celery sticks

2 red bell peppers

2 pounds fresh green beans

2 pints (or 2¼ pounds) cherry tomatoes

3 limes

1 honeydew melon (7 to 8 inch diameter melon)

2½ pounds fresh strawberries

Dairy

1 small piece Parmesan cheese (1 ounce needed for Parmesan curls)

Shopping List continued

Meat
8 (6-ounce) boneless, skinless chicken breasts

Grocery
1 small container pitted green or black olives (8 olives needed)

1 small jar horseradish

1 small package orzo

1 small container orange juice

1 small package powdered sugar

1 package ready-to-bake cookies

Staples
1 (6-ounce) can white tuna packed in water

Red onion

Lemons

Garlic

Cayenne pepper

Mayonnaise

No-sugar-added salad dressings such as oil (olive or canola) and vinegar with green onion

Canned black beans (16 ounces needed)

Olive oil

Balsamic vinegar

Salt

Black peppercorns

Spicy Tuna Spread

8 pitted green or black olives

1 (6-ounce) can white tuna packed in water

2 tablespoons mayonnaise

3 tablespoons horseradish

¼ cup fresh basil leaves, washed and dried

2 medium cucumbers, peeled and sliced on a diagonal

Place olives, tuna, mayonnaise, horseradish, and basil in a food processor and process until smooth. Taste for seasoning, adding more horseradish if necessary. Just before serving, spread on cucumber slices, and place on serving platter. Makes 8 servings.

Per serving: 49 calories, 6.3 grams protein, 3.8 grams carbohydrate, 1.3 grams fat (0.1 saturated), 9 milligrams cholesterol, 199 milligrams sodium, 0.6 gram fiber

No-Fuss Salad Bar

A colorful salad bar makes a pretty display and is easy to assemble. Here are some tips on how you can put one together without any washing or cutting. Buy a selection of these items in your market: prewashed lettuce, grated carrots, sliced red cabbage, celery sticks.

2 bags washed, ready-to-eat lettuce

4 cups shredded carrots

4 cups (1 bag) shredded red cabbage

4 cups celery sticks

4 cups cherry tomatoes, rinsed

8 tablespoons no-sugar-added salad dressing

All you need to do is open the bags and place the vegetables in attractive bowls. Add a bowl of cherry tomatoes. I have given you guidelines, but you can choose whatever vegetables you like. The secret is to make a colorful display. I like to use different sizes and shapes of bowls for the vegetables and dressing. For a party it's nice to fill bowls with the dressings. For nutritional values, plan 1 tablespoon dressing per person.

Buy 2 different types of dressings such as olive oil and balsamic vinegar, and green onion. Look for dressings that have no sugar added and are made with olive or canola oil.

Per serving: 139 calories, 3.1 grams protein, 14.9 grams carbohydrate, 8.8 grams fat (1.3 saturated), 0 milligram cholesterol, 182 milligrams sodium, 2.6 grams fiber

Lime Barbecued Chicken with Black Bean Sauce

½ cup fresh lime juice
1 cup olive oil
1 teaspoon cayenne pepper
4 garlic cloves, crushed, divided use
8 (6-ounce) boneless, skinless chicken breasts
¼ cup balsamic vinegar
½ cup orange juice
2 cups cooked black beans, drained and rinsed
Salt and freshly ground black pepper
¼ cup chopped red onion
2 red bell peppers, diced (2 cups)
Several sprigs fresh cilantro or parsley, for garnish

To prepare the chicken, mix lime juice, oil, cayenne pepper, and 2 cloves crushed garlic together and pour into plastic bag or bowl. Add the chicken breasts and marinate overnight or about 8 hours. Remove from refrigerator, drain, and bring to room temperature. Seal the juices in the chicken by browning each piece on both sides, about 2 minutes per side. Move chicken to a cooler area of grill to finish cooking without burning, about 5 minutes.

To prepare Black Bean Sauce, mix vinegar, orange juice, remaining 2 cloves garlic, and black beans together and purée in a blender or food processor. Add salt and pepper to taste. Warm in a microwave or in a saucepan. To blanch the onion and red pepper, bring a pot of water to the boil and add the onion and red pepper. As soon as the water returns to the boil, drain and rinse under cold water. An alternate preparation is to place onion and red pepper in a microwave-safe bowl and microwave on high for 3 minutes and immediately drain and rinse under cold water.

To serve, spoon a little Black Bean Sauce on a serving platter and place the chicken over the sauce. Sprinkle the top with the onion and red pepper. Garnish the platter with cilantro or parsley. Serve the remaining sauce on the side. Makes 8 servings.

Per serving: 353 calories, 54.0 grams protein, 15.2 grams carbohydrate, 9.3 grams fat (1.9 saturated), 132 milligrams cholesterol, 117 milligrams sodium, 1.8 grams fiber

Green Beans and Orzo Salad

1¼ cups orzo

2 pounds fresh green beans, trimmed and cut into 1-inch pieces (8 cups)

¼ cup no-sugar-added oil (olive or canola) and vinegar dressing

Salt and freshly ground black pepper

1 ounce Parmesan cheese (3 tablespoons sliced)

Bring a large pot with 3 to 4 quarts of water to a boil over high heat. Add the orzo and boil 5 minutes. Add the beans and continue to boil 5 minutes. Drain. Place in a serving bowl and drizzle the dressing on top and toss well. Add salt and pepper to taste. Make Parmesan curls by thinly slicing the Parmesan with a potato peeler. Place the curls on top of the salad. The salad may be served warm or at room temperature. Makes 8 servings.

Per serving: 224 calories, 7.2 grams protein, 30.0 grams carbohydrate, 10.1 grams fat (2.6 saturated), 3 milligrams cholesterol, 108 milligrams sodium, 3.4 grams fiber

Helpful Hints

- Orzo is rice-shaped pasta.

Melon with Marinated Strawberry Sauce and Hot Cookies

Melon with Marinated Strawberry Sauce

1 honeydew melon (7- to 8-inch diameter) sliced

2½ pounds fresh strawberries (8 cups)

¼ cup powdered sugar

2 tablespoons freshly squeezed lemon juice

8 hot cookies

Wash, hull, and slice strawberries. Blend in sugar and lemon juice. Let marinate 3 to 4 hours.

Place 2 slices melon on each dessert plate and spoon strawberry sauce on top. Serve 1 cookie on the side of each plate.

Makes 8 servings.

Per serving: 126 calories, 2.3 grams protein, 30.2 grams carbohydrate, 1 gram fat (0 saturated), 0 milligram cholesterol, 16 milligrams sodium, 3.3 grams fiber

Hot Cookies

Hot cookies just out of the oven are always welcome. Many markets sell freshly baked cookies. Or buy frozen cookie dough and bake the cookies just before dessert is served. They take only 10 to 12 minutes and everyone will enjoy the aroma.

8 ready-to-bake cookies

Preheat oven to 400 degrees. Separate 8 cookies and place about 2 inches apart on a cookie sheet. Bake 10 to 12 minutes. Remove to a rack to cool slightly before serving.

Makes 8 servings.

Per serving: 59 calories, 0.6 grams protein, 8.2 grams carbohydrate, 2.7 grams fat (0.9 saturated), 3.2 milligrams cholesterol, 28 milligrams sodium, 0.2 gram fiber

index

The first part of the key in **Bold** means: **QS**-Quick Start, **WC**=Which Carbs, **RC**=Right Carbs
The second part tells you: B=Breakfast, L=Lunch, D=Dinner (or supper), DS=Dessert

category index

acknowledgments

This book could not have been written without the patience and help of my husband, Harold. From the minute his cardiologist suggested he adopt a low-carbohydrate lifestyle seven years ago, he has helped me to create and test these recipes. Many thanks and much love.

Once again my assistant, Jackie Murrill, spent hours helping me test the recipes, and always with a smile. Thank you, Jackie, for your friendship and help.

At Bay Books, James Connolly, president, and Bill Schwartz, publisher, have worked endlessly and with great enthusiasm to bring this book to print. Thank you both for helping to bring my words to life. Thank you also, Floyd Yearout, my editor at Bay Books. You've been a delight to work with.

Lisa Ekus has been my trusted friend for many years and as my agent was a wonderful help in bringing my ideas to the page. Many thanks, Lisa.

I'd also like to thank my family who have always supported my projects and encouraged me every step of the way: My son James, his wife, Patty, and their sons, Zachary and Jacob, who helped taste these recipes; my son Charles and his wife, Lori, who tested recipes via e-mail; my son John, his wife, Jill, and their children, Jeffrey and Joanna, cheered me on; and my sister Roberta and brother-in-law Robert who helped to edit my thoughts and words.

Thanks go to Kathy Martin, my editor at the *Miami Herald,* who has been a friend and booster for my columns and books.

Thank you to Joseph Cooper, radio manager for WLRN National Public Radio for South Florida, who has helped and encouraged me with my "Food News and Views" segment on his program, *Topical Currents.*

I'd like to thank the many readers who correspond with me from all over the U.S. to say how much they enjoy the recipes and how much better they feel. This kind of encouragement makes the lonely time in front of the computer worthwhile.

Most important, I'd like to thank all of you who read this book and prepare the meals. I hope you enjoy them and reap the benefits as much as I've enjoyed creating the recipes and watching the wonderful results.